Cozy Cabin Quilts

from Thimbleberries®

20 PROJECTS FOR ANY HOME

LYNETTE JENSEN

C&T PUBLISHING

© 2002 Lynette Jensen

Editor-in-Chief: Darra Williamson

Editor: Jan Grigsby

Technical Editor: Joyce Engels Lytle, Sue Bahr

Copyeditor/Proofreader: Carol Barrett

Cover Designer: Aliza Kahn Shalit

Book Designer: C&T Publishing

Design Director: C&T Publishing

Graphic Illustrations: Lisa Kirchoff

Production Assistant: Jeffery Carrillo

Photography: All full page project quilts as well as ambience shots on pages 38, 42, 64, 90, 91, 114, 133 photographed by Keith Evenson. Other ambience shots by Diane Pedersen and Amy Marson. Stock photography provided by PhotoSpin unless otherwise noted.

Front Cover Image: *Double Star Crossing* by Lynette Jensen

Back Cover Image: *Bear Paw Scramble* and *Scrap Bag Sampler Quilt* by Lynette Jensen

Library of Congress Cataloging-in-Publication Data
Jensen, Lynette.
  Cozy Cabin Quilts from Thimbleberries : 20 Projects for Any Home / Lynette Jensen.
    p. cm.
  Includes index.
  ISBN 1-57120-176-9 (paper trade)
  1. Patchwork--Patterns. 2. Quilting--Patterns.
  3. Patchwork quilts. I. Thimbleberries, Inc. II. Title.
  TT835 .J453 2002
  746.46'041--dc21

                    2002006449

Published by C&T Publishing, Inc.
P.O. Box 1456
Lafayette, CA 94549
Printed in China
10 9 8 7 6 5 4 3 2 1

As long as I can remember, my family and friends have gone up North . . . to the lake . . . to the cottage . . . to the cabin or perhaps the hunting lodge. Today the lure of casual, comfortable living spaces has spilled over into our everyday lives. It is no longer necessary to have another dwelling to create the warmth and easy living atmosphere associated with cabin life, and more and more families are incorporating cozy, casual elements into their homes.

There has always been a general feeling and attitude about cabin life that makes us long for a weekend away. Soft comfortable clothes, easy overstuffed furniture and a general leisurely pace are all so very appealing. No wonder we all want to create this wonderful ambiance in our homes.

The casual style of cabin quilts can be recreated in your daily life by adding cabin-like elements to each and every room, and quilts are a natural. They add color, texture, softness, and warmth—both visual and physical comfort. The overall comfort of this casual lifestyle is reflected in the easy-to-make quilts throughout this book—quilts for beds, big and small. Smaller quilts visually add "warmth" to walls and table tops. Lap quilts are likely to be the quilts most loved and appreciated by those who want to cuddle up on the couch to read, watch television, or take a Sunday afternoon nap.

Whether your dream retreat is a snowy mountain ski cabin, a lakeside cottage, a retreat in the woods, or perhaps an oceanside hideaway, *Cozy Cabin Quilts from Thimbleberries* will help you create a warm, inviting atmosphere no matter where you live.

Introduction

Contents

The cabin is ready. Car doors slam, sleepy children tumble awake ("are we there yet?"), grown-ups laugh and hug hello. The season for family reunions is here. Why not capture the "warm fuzzies" in a special quilt?

Family Reunion

Pack *permanent* pens, rubber stamps—even fabric paint—to record signatures, handprints, and other *family memories*.

"A *cherished* quilt provides the perfect backdrop for a *joyful* family gathering."

family Album Quilt

64" x 76"

Block: 4" square (finished)

Fabrics and Supplies

Yardage based on 42"-wide fabric

- 1⅝ yards **blue print** for album blocks
- 1 yard **beige print** for album blocks
- 1⅛ yards **red floral** for horizontal lattice strips and pieced border
- 1¼ yards **red print** for vertical lattice strips and pieced border
- ⅝ yard **gold print** for inner border and corner squares
- 1⅝ yards **blue floral** for outer border
- ¾ yard **red/blue diagonal print** for binding
- 4 yards backing fabric
- Quilt batting, at least 68" x 80"

Album Blocks

Make 63 blocks.

CUTTING

From blue print:

Cut seven 4½" x 42" strips. From these strips cut sixty-three 4½" squares.

Cut seven 2" x 42" strips. From these strips cut 126–2" squares.

From beige print:

Cut ten 3" x 42" strips. From these strips cut 126–3" squares.

PIECING

Step 1

Position a 3" **beige** square on the lower left corner of a 4½" **blue** square. Draw a diagonal line on the **beige** square and stitch on the line. Trim the seam allowance to ¼" and press. Repeat this process at the opposite corner of the **blue** square. *At this point each square should measure 4½" square.*

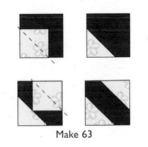

Make 63

Step 2

Position a 2" **blue** square on the lower left corner of a Step 1 square. Draw a diagonal line on the **blue** square and stitch on the line. Trim the seam allowance to ¼" and press. Repeat this process at the opposite corner of the Step 1 square. *At this point each square should measure 4½" square.*

Make 63

Quilt Center

CUTTING

From red floral:

Cut seven 2½" x 42" strips. From these strips cut fifty-six 2½" x 4½" horizontal lattice strips.

From red print:

Cut nine 2½" x 42" strips. Diagonally piece the strips as needed. From these strips cut six 2½" x 52½" vertical lattice strips.

QUILT CENTER ASSEMBLY

Step 1

Referring to the quilt diagram for placement, lay out the album blocks, **red floral** horizontal lattice strips, and **red print** vertical lattice strips. Sew the album blocks and the 2½" x 4½" **red floral** horizontal lattice strips together in rows and press. Make 7 block rows. *At this point each block row should measure 4½" x 52½".*

Step 2

Referring to the quilt diagram for placement, pin and sew together the block rows and the 2½" x 52½" **red print** vertical lattice strips. Press the seam allowances toward the lattice strips. *At this point the quilt center should measure 40½" x 52½".*

Borders

NOTE: The yardage given allows for the border strips to be cut on the crosswise grain. Diagonally piece the strips as needed, referring to page 140 for Diagonal Piecing instructions.

CUTTING

From **gold print:**

Cut one 4½" x 42" strip. From this strip cut four 4½" corner squares.

Cut five 2½" x 42" inner border strips.

From **red floral:**

Cut six 2½" x 42" strips.

From **red print:**

Cut six 2½" x 42" strips.

From **blue floral:**

Cut eight 6½" x 42" outer border strips.

ATTACHING THE BORDERS

Step 1

To attach the 2½"-wide **gold** inner border strips, refer to page 139 for Border instructions.

Step 2

Aligning long edges, sew the 2½" x 42" **red floral** and **red print** strips together in pairs. Press, referring to page 138 for Hints and Helps for Pressing Strip Sets. Make a total of 6 strip sets. Cut the strip sets into segments.

4½"   4½"

Crosscut 50 segments

Step 3

For the top and bottom pieced borders, sew together 11 of the Step 2 segments and press. *At this point each pieced border should measure 4½" x 44½".* Sew the border strips to the quilt center and press.

Make 2

Step 4

For the side pieced borders, sew together 14 of the Step 2 segments and press. Make 2 border strips. *At this point each pieced border should measure 4½" x 56½".*

Sew 4½" **gold** corner squares to both ends of the border strips and press. Sew the border strips to the quilt center and press.

Make 2

Step 5

To attach the 6½"-wide **blue floral** outer border strips, refer to page 139 for Border instructions.

Putting It All Together

Cut the 4-yard length of backing fabric in half crosswise to make two 2-yard lengths. Refer to Finishing the Quilt on page 139 for complete instructions.

Binding

CUTTING

From **red/blue diagonal print:**

Cut eight 2¾" x 42" strips.

Sew the binding to the quilt using a ⅜" seam allowance. This measurement will produce a ½"-wide finished double binding. Refer to page 140 for Diagonal Piecing and Binding instructions.

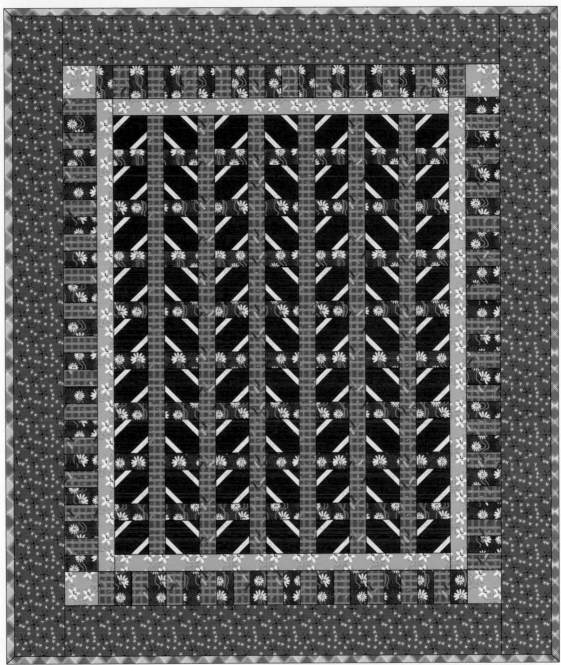

Family Album Quilt Diagram, 64" x 76"

Hourglass quilt

80¼" x 96½"

Block: 3¼" square (finished)

Fabrics and Supplies

Yardage based on 42"-wide fabric

- 2 yards **red print** for Hourglass blocks and middle border
- 3 yards **cream print** for Hourglass blocks
- 1½ yards **beige grid** for Hourglass blocks
- 1 yard **green print** for inner border
- 2⅞ yards **beige floral** for outer border
- ⅞ yard **red/green diagonal print** for binding
- 7⅛ yards backing fabric
- Quilt batting, at least 85" x 100"

Hourglass Blocks

Make 187 **red/cream** blocks.

Make 187 **beige grid/cream** blocks.

CUTTING

From red print:

Cut eleven 4½" x 42" strips. From these strips cut ninety-four 4½" squares. Cut the squares diagonally into quarters to make 376 triangles. You will be using 374 triangles.

From cream print:

Cut twenty-one 4½" x 42" strips. From these strips cut 187–4½" squares. Cut the squares diagonally into quarters to make 748 triangles.

From beige grid:

Cut eleven 4½" x 42" strips. From these strips cut ninety-four 4½" squares. Cut the squares diagonally into quarters to make 376 triangles. You will be using 374 triangles.

PIECING

Step 1

Layer a **red** triangle on a **cream** triangle. Stitch along the bias edge as shown, being careful not to stretch the triangles. Press the seam allowance toward the **red** triangle. Repeat for all remaining **red** triangles and 374 **cream** triangles, stitching along the same bias edge of each triangle set. Sew the triangle units together in pairs and press. *At this point each Hourglass block should measure 3¾" square.*

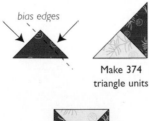

bias edges

Make 374 triangle units

Make 187 Hourglass blocks

Step 2

Layer a **cream** triangle on a **beige grid** triangle. Stitch along the bias edge as shown, being careful not to stretch the triangles. Press the seam allowance toward the **beige grid** triangle. Repeat for the remaining **cream** and **beige grid** triangles, stitching along the same bias edge of each triangle set. Sew the triangle units together in pairs and press. *At this point each Hourglass block should measure 3¾" square.*

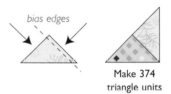

bias edges

Make 374 triangle units

Make 187 Hourglass blocks

Quilt Center

Step 1

Referring to the quilt diagram for the block placement, sew the Step 1 and Step 2 blocks together in 22 horizontal rows of 17 blocks each.

Press the seam allowances in alternating directions by rows so the seams will fit snugly together with less bulk.

Step 2

Pin the rows at the block intersections and sew the rows together. Press the seam allowances in one

direction. *At this point the quilt center should measure 55¾" x 72".*

Borders

NOTE: The yardage given allows for the inner and middle border strips to be cut on the crosswise grain. Diagonally piece the strips as needed, referring to page 140 for Diagonal Piecing instructions. The yardage given for the **beige floral** outer border strips allows for these strips to be cut on the lengthwise grain.

CUTTING

From **green print**:
Cut eight 3½" x 42" inner border strips.

From **red print**:
Cut eight 2" x 42" middle border strips.

From **beige floral** (cut on the lengthwise grain):
Cut two 8½" x 100" side outer border strips.

Cut two 8½" x 70" top/bottom outer border strips.

ATTACHING THE BORDERS

Step 1
To attach the 3½"-wide **green print** inner border strips, refer to page 139 for Border instructions.

Step 2
To attach the 2"-wide **red print** middle border strips, refer to page 139 for Border instructions.

Step 3
To attach the 8½"-wide **beige floral** outer border strips, refer to page 139 for Border instructions.

Putting It All Together

Cut the 7⅛-yard length of backing fabric in thirds crosswise to form three 2⅜-yard lengths. Refer to Finishing the Quilt on page 139 for complete instructions.

Binding

CUTTING

From **red/green diagonal print**:
Cut ten 2¾" x 42" strips.

Sew the binding to the quilt using a ⅜" seam allowance. This measurement will produce a ½"-wide finished double binding. Refer to page 140 for Diagonal Piecing and Binding instructions.

Hourglass Quilt Diagram, 84¼" x 96½"

Patchwork *fare*

Patchwork fare

64"x 78"

Fabrics and Supplies

Yardage based on 42"-wide fabric

- 1¾ yards **beige print** for quilt center and pieced outer border
- ¾ yard **blue print** for triangle blocks
- 1¼ yards **red print** for lattice and pieced outer border
- ⅜ yard **gold plaid** for lattice posts and triangle block corner squares
- 1⅔ yards **dark blue print** for inner border and pieced outer border
- ⅔ yard **dark blue print** for binding
- 4 yards backing fabric
- Quilt batting, at least 68" x 82"

Quilt Center

CUTTING

From beige print:

Cut one 13¼" x 42" strip. From this strip cut one 13¼" square. Cut the square diagonally into quarters to make 4 large triangles. From the remainder of the strip, cut two 9¼" squares. Cut the squares diagonally into quarters to make 8 small triangles.

Cut two 8½" x 42" strips. From these strips cut six 8½" x 12½" rectangles.

From blue print:

Cut one 13¼" x 42" strip. From this strip cut one 13¼" square. Cut the square diagonally into quarters to make 4 large triangles. From the remainder of the strip cut two 9¼" squares. Cut the squares diagonally into quarters to make 8 small triangles.

From red print:

Cut five 2½" x 42" strips. From these strips cut seven 2½" x 12½" lattice strips and ten 2½" x 8½" lattice strips.

From gold plaid:

Cut one 2½" x 42" strip. From this strip cut six 2½" lattice post squares.

PIECING

Step 1

Layer a large **beige** triangle on a large **blue** triangle. Stitch along the bias edge as shown, being careful not to stretch the triangles. Press the seam allowance toward the **blue** triangle. Repeat for the remaining large **beige** and **blue** triangles stitching along the same bias edge of each triangle set so that your pieced triangle units will all have the **beige** triangles on the same side. Sew the triangle units together in pairs, and press.

At this point each large triangle block should measure 12½" square.

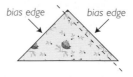

Make 4 triangle units

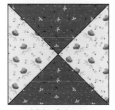
Make 2 large triangle blocks

Step 2

Layer a small **beige** triangle on a small **blue** triangle. Stitch along the bias edge as shown, being careful not to stretch the triangles. Press the seam allowance toward the **blue** triangle. Repeat for the remaining small **beige** and **blue** triangles stitching along the same bias edge of each triangle set so that your pieced triangle units will all have the **beige** triangles on the same side. Sew the triangle units together in pairs, and press.

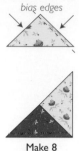

At this point each small triangle block should measure 8½" square.

bias edges

Make 8
triangle units

Make 4 small
triangle blocks

Step 3

Sew 2½" x 8½" **red** lattice strips to both ends of an 8½" x 12½" **beige** rectangle, and press. Sew 2 of the Step 2 small triangle blocks to both ends of the unit and press. *At this point each section should measure 8½" x 32½".*

Make 2

Step 4

Sew 2½" **gold plaid** lattice post squares to both ends of a 2½" x 12½" **red** lattice strip and press. Sew 2½" x 8½" **red** lattice strips to both ends of the unit and press. *At this point each lattice strip should measure 2½" x 32½".*

Make 3

Step 5

Sew 2½" x 12½" **red** lattice strips to both sides of a large triangle block and press. Sew 8½" x 12½" **beige** rectangles to both ends of the unit and press. *At this point each section should measure 12½" x 32½".*

Make 2

Step 6

Referring to the quilt center diagram, sew the Step 3, 4, and 5 sections together and press. *At this point the quilt center should measure 32½" x 46½".*

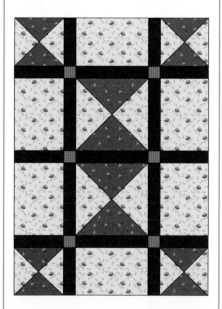

Borders

NOTE: The yardage given allows for the border strips to be cut on the crosswise grain. Diagonally piece the strips as needed, referring to page 140 for Diagonal Piecing instructions.

CUTTING

From **dark blue print:**
Cut six 8½" x 42" strips. From these strips cut two 8½" x 46½" side inner border strips, two 8½" x 32½" top/bottom inner border strips, and eight 8½" squares.

From **beige print:**
Cut three 8½" x 42" strips. From these strips cut two 8½" x 30½" strips and two 8½" x 16½" strips.

From **red print:**
Cut three 8½" x 42" strips. From these strips cut twelve 8½" squares.

From **gold plaid:**
Cut two 9¼" squares. Cut the squares diagonally into quarters to make 8 triangles.

From **blue print:**
Cut two 9¼" squares. Cut the squares diagonally into quarters to make 8 triangles.

PIECING

Step 1

Layer a **gold plaid** triangle on a **blue** triangle. Stitch along the bias edge as shown, being careful not to stretch the triangles. Press the seam allowance toward the **blue** triangle. Repeat for the remaining **gold plaid** and **blue** triangles, stitching along the same bias edge of each triangle set so that your pieced triangle units will all have the **gold plaid** triangles on the same side. Sew the triangle units together in pairs and press. *At this point each triangle block should measure 8½" square.*

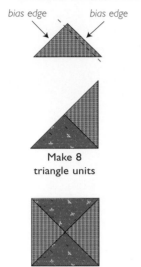

Make 8 triangle units

Make 4 triangle blocks

Step 2

Sew 8½" **red** squares to both ends of an 8½" x 16½" **beige** strip and press. Make 2 strips. Sew the strips to each of the 8½" x 32½" **dark blue** strips and press. Referring to the quilt diagram, sew the strips to the top/ bottom of the quilt center and press.

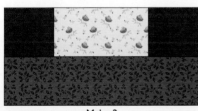

Make 2

Step 3

Referring to the quilt diagram, sew 8½" **red** squares to both ends of an 8½" x 30½" **beige** strip and press. Make 2 strips. Sew the strips to each of the 8½" x 46½" **dark blue** strips and press. Set the strips aside.

Step 4

Referring to the diagram for color placement, sew 8½" **dark blue** squares to the Step 1 triangle blocks. Press the seam allowances toward the **dark blue** squares. Sew the 8½" **dark blue** squares to the 8½" **red** squares. Press the seam allowances toward the **dark blue** squares. Sew the units together to make the corner squares. *At this point each corner square should measure 16½" square.*

( ) ( )

Make 2 each

Step 5

Referring to the quilt diagram, sew the pieced corner squares to both ends of the Step 3 strips and press. Make 2 strips. Sew the strips to the sides of the quilt center and press.

Putting It All Together

Cut the 4-yard length of backing fabric in half crosswise to make two 2-yard lengths. Refer to Finishing the Quilt on page 139 for complete instructions.

Binding

CUTTING

From **dark blue print**:
Cut eight 2¾" x 42" strips.

Sew the binding to the quilt using a ⅜" seam allowance. This measurement will produce a ½"-wide finished double binding. Refer to page 140 for Diagonal Piecing and Binding instructions.

Patchwork Fare Quilt Diagram, 64" x 78"

scrap bag
Sampler Quilt

scrap bag *Sampler Quilt*

34" x 44"
Block with border 10" square (finished)

Fabrics and Supplies

Yardage based on 42"-wide fabric

- ¼ yard each of six **assorted beige prints** for blocks (Number fabrics 1–6.)

OR

- 1 yard total of one **beige print** for blocks
- 3" x 20" piece **red print #1** for Garden Path block
- ⅛ yard **gold print #1** for Garden Path block and block border
- ⅛ yard **black print** for Double Star block and block border
- 3" x 20" piece **gold print #2** for Double Star block
- ⅛ yard **green grid** for December Pines block and block border
- ⅛ yard **green print #1** for December Pines block and block border
- 1½" x 5" piece **brown print** for December Pines block
- ⅛ yard **green print #2** for Indian Puzzle block and block border
- ⅛ yard **eggplant print** for Indian Puzzle block and block border

- 5" x 42" strip **red print #2** for Pinwheel Star block and block border
- 5" x 42" strip **gold print #3** for Pinwheel Star block and block border
- ⅛ yard **light blue print** for Flying Geese block and block border
- 6" x 42" strip **blue grid** for Flying Geese block and block border
- 3" x 42" strip **red print #3** for block border
- 3" x 42" strip **gold print #4** for block border
- ¼ yard **medium green** for inner border
- 1 yard **dark blue print** for outer border
- ⅜ yard **medium green print** for binding
- 1⅓ yards backing fabric
- Quilt batting, at least 38" x 48"

The cutting and piecing instructions for each block are listed separately.

Garden Path Block

CUTTING

From **red print #1**:
Cut one 2" x 20" strip. From this strip cut nine 2" squares.

From **gold print #1**:
Cut one 1⅝" x 20" strip. From this strip cut two 1⅝" squares and eight 1¼" x 2" rectangles.

From **beige print #1**:
Cut one 1⅝" x 20" strip. From this strip cut two 1⅝" squares and four 1¼" x 2" rectangles.

Cut two 1¼" x 20" strips. From these strips cut twenty-eight 1¼" squares.

From **green grid**:
Cut one 1½" x 42" inner block border strip.

From **black print**:
Cut one 1½" x 42" outer block border strip.

PIECING

Step 1

Position a 1¼" **beige** square on the corner of a 1¼" x 2" **gold** rectangle. Draw a diagonal line on the **beige** square and stitch on the line.

24   COZY CABIN QUILTS

Trim the seam allowance to ¼" and press. Repeat this process at the opposite corner of the **gold** rectangle. Make 2 units. Sew the units to the top and bottom of a 2" **red** square and press.

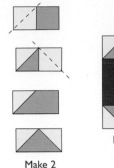

Make 2

Make 1

Step 2

Position a 1¼" x 2" **beige** rectangle on the left-hand corner of a 1¼" x 2" **gold** rectangle. Draw a diagonal line on the **beige** rectangle and stitch on the line. Trim the seam allowance to ¼" and press. Repeat this process at the opposite corner of the **gold** rectangle. Make 2 units. Sew the units to the sides of the Step 1 unit and press. *At this point the unit should measure 3½" square.*

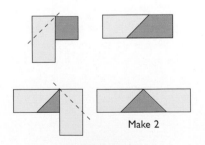

Make 2

Make 1

Step 3

Position a 1¼" **beige** square on the upper left corner of a 2" **red** square. Draw a diagonal line on the **beige** square and stitch on the line. Trim the seam allowance to ¼" and press. Repeat this process at the adjacent corner of the **red** square. Make 8 units. Sew the units together in pairs and press. Sew 2 of the units to both sides of the Step 2 unit and press. *At this point the unit should measure 3½" x 6½".*

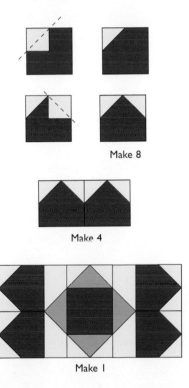

Make 8

Make 4

Make 1

Step 4

Position a 1¼" **beige** square on the left-hand corner of a 1¼" x 2" **gold** rectangle. Draw a diagonal line on the **beige** square and stitch on the line. Trim the seam allowance to ¼" and press.

Make 4

Step 5

With right sides together, layer the 1⅝" **gold** and **beige** squares together. Cut the layered squares in half diagonally to make 4 sets of triangles. Stitch ¼" from the diagonal edge of each set of triangles and press. *At this point each triangle-pieced square should measure 1¼" square.* Sew a 1¼" **beige** square to the left-hand side of each triangle-pieced square and press.

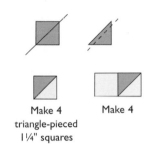

Make 4 triangle-pieced 1¼" squares

Make 4

Step 6

Sew the Step 4 and Step 5 units together in pairs and press. Sew the units to both sides of the 2 remaining Step 3 units and press. *At this point each unit should measure 2" x 6½".*

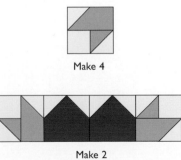

Make 4

Make 2

Step 7

Referring to the block diagram, sew the 3 horizontal rows together and press. *At this point the Garden Path block should measure 6½" square.*

Garden Path block

Step 8

To attach the 1½"-wide **green grid** inner block border, refer to Border instructions on page 139.

Step 9

To attach the 1½"-wide **black** outer block border, refer to Border instructions on page 139. *At this point the block should measure 10½" square.*

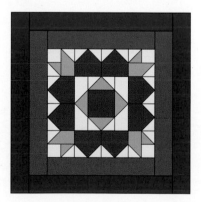

Double Star Block

CUTTING

From **black print**:

Cut one 1⅝" x 12" strip.

Cut one 1¼" x 12" strip. From this strip cut eight 1¼" squares.

From **beige print #2**:

Cut one 2" x 16" strip. From this strip cut four 2" x 3½" rectangles.

Cut one 1⅝" x 12" strip.

Cut one 1¼" x 42" strip. From this strip cut four 1¼" x 2" rectangles and fourteen 1¼" squares.

From **gold print #2**:

Cut one 2" x 20" strip. From this strip cut eight 2" squares.

From **green print #1**:

Cut one 1½" x 42" inner block border strip.

From **red print #2**:

Cut one 1½" x 42" outer block border strip.

PIECING

Step 1

With right sides together, layer the 1⅝" x 12" **black** and **beige** strips. Press together, but do not sew. Cut the layered strips into squares. Cut the layered squares in half diagonally to make 10 sets of triangles. Stitch ¼" from the diagonal edge of each set of triangles and press. *At this point each triangle-pieced square should measure 1¼" square.*

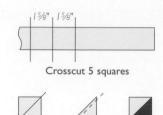

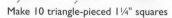

Crosscut 5 squares

Make 10 triangle-pieced 1¼" squares

Step 2

Sew the triangle-pieced squares and 1¼" **beige** squares together in pairs and press. Sew the pairs together and press. *At this point each unit should measure 2" square.*

Make 5

Step 3

Position a 1¼" **black** square on the corner of a 1¼" x 2" **beige** rectangle. Draw a diagonal line on the **black** square and stitch on the line. Trim the seam allowance to ¼" and press. Repeat this process at the opposite corner of the **beige** rectangle. *At this point each star point unit should measure 1¼" x 2".*

Make 4
star point units

Step 4

Sew Step 3 star point units to the top and bottom of the Step 2 unit and press. Sew 1¼" **beige** squares to both ends of the remaining star point units and press. Sew the units to both sides of the square and press.

At this point the pieced center block should measure 3½" square.

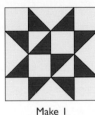

Make 1
center block

Step 5

Position a 2" **gold** square on the corner of a 2" x 3½" **beige** rectangle. Draw a diagonal line on the **gold** square and stitch on the line. Trim the seam allowance to ¼" and press. Repeat this process at the opposite corner of the **beige** rectangle. *At this point each star point unit should measure 2" x 3½".*

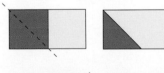

Make 4
star point units

Step 6

Sew 2 of the Step 5 star point units to both sides of the Step 4 center

block and press. *At this point the unit should measure 3½" x 6½".*

Make 1

Step 7

Sew the Step 2 units to both sides of the 2 remaining Step 5 star point units and press. *At this point the unit should measure 2" x 6½".*

Make 2

Step 8

Referring to the block diagram, sew the 3 horizontal rows together and press. *At this point the Double Star block should measure 6½" square.*

Double Star block

Step 9

To attach the 1½"-wide **green #1** inner block border, refer to Border instructions on page 139.

Step 10

To attach the 1½"-wide **red #2** outer block border, refer to Border instructions on page 139. *At this point the block should measure 10½" square.*

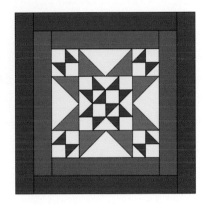

December Pines Block

CUTTING

From green grid:

Cut one 1½" x 14" strip. From this strip cut five 1½" x 2½" rectangles.

From green print #1:

Cut one 1½" x 22" strip. From this strip cut eight 1½" x 2½" rectangles.

From beige print #3:

Cut two 1½" x 29" strips. From these strips cut two 1½" x 3½" rectangles, twenty-four 1½" squares, and two 1¼" x 5" strips.

From brown print:

Cut one 1¼" x 5" strip.

From gold print #3:

Cut one 1½" x 42" inner block border strip.

From red print #3:

Cut one 1½" x 42" outer block border strip.

PIECING

Step 1

Position a 1½" x 3½" **beige** rectangle on the left-hand corner of a 1½" x 2½" **green grid** rectangle. Draw a diagonal line on the **beige** rectangle and stitch on the line. Trim the seam allowance to ¼" and press. Repeat this process at the adjacent corner of the **green grid** rectangle.

At this point the unit should measure 1½" x 6½".

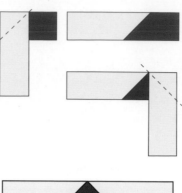

Make 1 tree top

Step 2

Position a 1½" **beige** square on the corner of a 1½" x 2½" **green grid** rectangle. Draw a diagonal line on the **beige** square and stitch on the line. Trim the seam allowance to ¼" and press. Repeat this process at the opposite corner of the **green grid** rectangle. Sew the units together to make 1 tree section. Press the seam allowances toward the top of the section. *At this point the section should measure 2½" x 4½".*

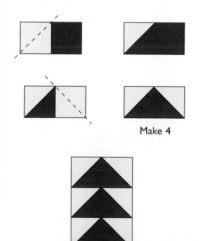

Make 4

Make 1 tree section

Step 3

Position a 1½" **beige** square on the corner of a 1½" x 2½" **green print** rectangle. Draw a diagonal line on the **beige** square and stitch on the line. Trim the seam allowance to ¼" and press. Repeat this process at the opposite corner of the **green print** rectangle. Make 8 units. Sew the units together to make 2 tree sections with 4 units each. Press the seam allowances toward the bottom of the sections. *At this point each section should measure 2½" x 4½".*

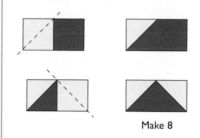

Make 8

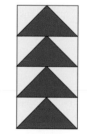

Make 2 tree section

Step 4

Sew the Step 3 tree sections to both sides of the Step 2 tree section and press. *At this point the unit should measure 4½" x 6½".*

Make 1

Step 5

Aligning long edges, sew a 1¼" x 5" **beige** strip to both sides of the 1" x 5" **brown** strip and press. Cut the strip set into segments. Referring to the block diagram sew the segments together to make the trunk section. *At this point the trunk section should measure 1½" x 6½".*

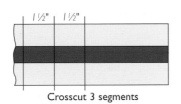

Crosscut 3 segments

Step 6

Referring to the block diagram, sew the 3 horizontal rows together and press. *At this point the December Pines block should measure 6½" square.*

December Pines block

Step 7

To attach the 1½"-wide **gold #3** inner block border, refer to Border instructions on page 139.

Step 8

To attach the 1½"-wide **red #3** outer block border, refer to Border instructions on page 139. *At this point the block should measure 10½" square.*

Indian Puzzle Block

CUTTING

From **green print #2**:
Cut one 1½" x 24" strip. From this strip cut four 1½" x 2½" rectangles and eight 1½" squares.

From **eggplant print**:
Cut one 1⅞" x 15" strip.

Cut four 1½" squares.

From **beige print #4**:
Cut one 1⅞" x 15" strip.

Cut one 1½" x 42" strip. From this strip cut six 1½" x 2½" rectangles and twelve 1½" squares.

From **light blue print**:
Cut one 1½" x 42" inner block border strip.

From **gold print #1**:
Cut one 1½" x 42" outer block border strip.

PIECING

Step 1

Position a 1½" **green** square on the corner of a 1½" x 2½" **beige** rectangle. Draw a diagonal line on the **green** square and stitch on the line. Trim the seam allowance to ¼" and press. Repeat this process at the opposite corner of the **beige** rectangle.

Make 4

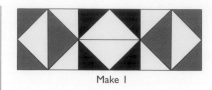

Step 2

Position a 1½" **beige** square on the corner of a 1½" x 2½" **green** rectangle. Draw a diagonal line on the **beige** square, stitch, trim the seam allowance to ¼", and press. Repeat this process at the opposite corner of the **green** rectangle.

Make 4

Step 3

Sew the Step 1 unit to the top of the Step 2 unit and press. *At this point each unit should measure 2½" square.*

Make 4

Step 4

Position a 1½" **eggplant** square on the corner of a 1½" x 2½" **beige** rectangle. Draw a diagonal line on the **eggplant** square, stitch, trim the seam allowance, and press. Repeat this process at the opposite corner of the **beige** rectangle. Make 2 units. Sew the units together and press. Sew 2 of the Step 3 units to both sides of this unit and press. *At this point the unit should measure 2½" x 6½".*

Make 2

Make 1

Make 1

Step 5

With right sides together, layer together the 1⅞" x 15" **beige** and **eggplant** strips. Press together, but do not sew. Cut the layered strips into squares. Cut the layered squares in half diagonally to make 12 sets of triangles. Stitch ¼" from the diagonal edge of each set of triangles and press. *At this point each triangle-pieced square should measure 1½" square.*

Crosscut 6 squares

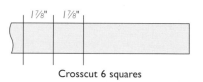

Make 12 triangle-pieced 1½" squares

Step 6

Referring to the diagram, sew 3 triangle-pieced squares and a 1½" **beige** square together and press. Make 4 units. Sew the units to both sides of the 2 remaining Step 3 units and press. *At this point each unit should measure 2½" x 6½".*

Make 4

Make 2

Step 7

Referring to the block diagram, sew the 3 horizontal rows together and press. *At this point the Indian Puzzle block should measure 6½" square.*

Indian Puzzle block

Step 8

To attach the 1½"-wide **light blue** inner block border, refer to Border instructions on page 139.

Step 9

To attach the 1½"-wide **gold #1** outer block border, refer to Border instructions on page 139. *At this point the block should measure 10½" square.*

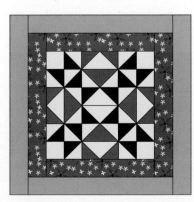

Pinwheel Star Block

CUTTING

From **red print #2**:
Cut one 2¾" square, cutting it diagonally into quarters to make 4 triangles.

From **beige print #5**:
Cut one 2¾" x 42" strip. From this strip cut one 2¾" square, cutting it diagonally into quarters to make 4 triangles, four 2" x 3½" rectangles, and four 2" squares.

From **gold print #3**:
Cut two 2⅜" squares. Cut the squares in half diagonally to make 4 triangles.

Cut eight 2" squares.

From **blue grid**:
Cut one 1½" x 42" inner block border strip.

From **gold print #4**:
Cut one 1½" x 42" outer block border strip.

PIECING

Step 1

Layer a **red** triangle on a **beige** triangle. Stitch along the bias edge as shown, being careful not to stretch the triangles and press. Repeat for the remaining **red** and **beige** triangles, stitching along the same bias edge of each triangle set so the pieced triangle units will have the **red** triangle on the same side.

bias edges

Make 4

Step 2

Sew a **gold** triangle to each of the Step 1 units and press. Sew the units together in pairs and press. Referring to the diagram, sew the unit pairs together and press. *At this point the pieced square should measure 3½" square.*

Make 4   Make 2

Make 1

Step 3

Position a 2" **gold** square on the corner of a 2" x 3½" **beige** rectangle. Draw a diagonal line on the **gold** square and stitch on the line. Trim the seam allowance to ¼" and press. Repeat this process at the opposite corner of the **beige** rectangle.

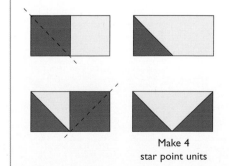

Make 4
star point units

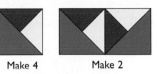

Step 4

Sew 2 of the Step 3 star point units to both sides of the Step 2 square and press. *At this point the unit should measure 3½" x 6½".*

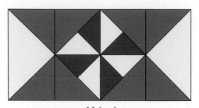

Make 1

Step 5

Sew 2" **beige** squares to both sides of the remaining star point units and press. *At this point the unit should measure 2" x 6½".*

Make 2

Step 6

Referring to the block diagram, sew the 3 horizontal rows together and press. *At this point the Pinwheel Star block should measure 6½" square.*

Pinwheel Star block

Step 7

To attach the 1½"-wide **blue grid** inner block border, refer to Border instructions on page 139.

Step 8

To attach the 1½"-wide **gold #4** outer block border, refer to Border instructions on page 139. *At this point the block should measure 10½" square.*

Flying Geese Block

CUTTING

From **light blue print**:
Cut one 1¼" x 42" strip. From this strip cut sixteen 1¼" x 2" rectangles.

From **beige print #6**:
Cut one 4¼" square, cutting it diagonally into quarters to make 4 triangles. You will be using only 2 triangles.

Cut one 1¼" x 42" strip. From this strip cut thirty-two 1¼" squares.

Cut two 2⅜" squares.

From **blue grid**:
Cut one 4¼" square, cutting it diagonally into quarters to make 4 triangles. You will use only 2 of the triangles.

Cut two 2⅜" squares.

From **green print #2**:
Cut one 1½" x 42" inner block border strip.

From **eggplant print**:
Cut one 1½" x 42" outer block border strip.

PIECING

Step 1

Position a 1¼" **beige** square on the corner of a 1¼" x 2" **light blue** rectangle. Draw a diagonal line on the **beige** square and stitch on the line. Trim the seam allowance to ¼" and press. Repeat this process at the opposite corner of the **light blue** rectangle. Sew 4 of the flying geese units together and press. *At this point each four-piece unit should measure 2" x 3½".*

Make 16
flying geese units

Make 4
four-piece units

Step 2

With right sides together, layer a **beige** triangle on a **blue grid** triangle. Stitch along the bias edge as shown, being careful not to stretch the triangles and press. Repeat for the remaining **beige** and **blue grid** triangles, stitching along the same bias edge of each triangle set so the pieced triangle units will all have the **beige** triangle on the same side. Sew the triangle units together and press. *At this point the triangle block should measure 3½" square.*

Sew 2 of the Step 1 four-piece units to both sides of the triangle block and press. *At this point the unit should measure 3½" x 6½".*

bias edge   bias edge

Make 2   Make 1

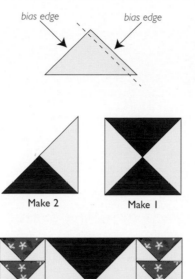

Step 3

With right sides together, layer the 2⅜" **blue grid** and **beige** squares in pairs. Press together, but do not sew. Cut the layered squares in half diagonally to make 4 sets of triangles. Stitch ¼" from the diagonal edge of each set of triangles, and press to make 4 triangle-pieced squares. Sew the triangle-pieced squares to both sides of the remain-

ing Step 1 four-piece units and press. *At this point each unit should measure 2" x 6½".*

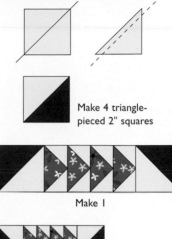

Make 4 triangle-pieced 2" squares

Make 1

Make 1

Step 4

Referring to the block diagram, sew the 3 horizontal rows together and press.

At this point the Flying Geese block should measure 6½" square.

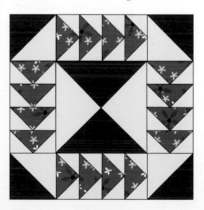

Step 5

To attach the 1½"-wide **green #2** inner block border, refer to Border instructions on page 139.

Step 6

To attach the 1½"-wide **eggplant** outer block border, refer to Border instructions on page 139. *At this point the block should measure 10½" square.*

Quilt Center

Step 1

Referring to the quilt diagram, sew the blocks together in 2 rows of 3 blocks each. Press the seam allowances in alternating directions by rows so the seams will fit snugly together with less bulk.

Step 2

Pin the rows at the block intersections and sew the rows together. Press the seam allowances in one direction. *At this point the quilt center should measure 20½" x 30½".*

Borders

NOTE: The yardage given allows for the border strips to be cut on the crosswise grain. Diagonally piece the strips as needed, referring to page 140 for Diagonal Piecing instructions.

CUTTING

From **medium green print**:
Cut three 1½" x 42" inner border strips.

From **dark blue print**:
Cut five 6½" x 42" outer border strips.

ATTACHING THE BORDERS

Step 1

To attach the 1½"-wide **medium green** inner border strips, refer to page 139 for Border instructions.

Step 2

To attach the 6½"-wide **dark blue** outer border strips, refer to page 139 for Border instructions.

Putting It All Together

Trim the batting and backing so they are 4" larger than the quilt top. Refer to Finishing the Quilt on page 139 for complete instructions.

Binding

CUTTING

From **medium green print**:
Cut four 2¾" x 42" strips.

Sew the binding to the quilt using a ⅜" seam allowance. This measurement will produce a ½"-wide finished double binding. Refer to page 140 for Diagonal Piecing and Binding instructions.

Scrap Bag Sampler Quilt Diagram, 34" x 44"

Whether buried deep in the woods, perched on a hillside, or overlooking the sea, a cabin offers the perfect opportunity to reconnect with nature. Don't forget a cozy quilt for those crisp autumn evenings.

Nature

Can you *imagine*
a soundtrack more
glorious than nature?

"Tangy *apple cider*, the pungent aroma of wood smoke, a mellow mix of cloth and comfort: *life is good.*"

bird *Watching* throw
68" x 76"

Fabrics and Supplies

Yardage based on 42"-wide fabric

- ⅞ yard **beige print** for background, flying geese units, and triangle blocks
- 1 yard **dark green print** for tree and three borders
- ¾ yard **medium green print** for tree, two borders, and triangle blocks
- ¼ yard **brown print** for tree trunk and corner squares
- ¼ yard **blue print #1** for roof and triangle blocks
- ⅞ yard **red print** for house, flying geese units, triangle blocks, and checkerboard
- ½ yard **gold print** for house, triangle blocks, and checkerboard
- ⅜ yard **blue print #2** for block border, triangle blocks, and birdhouse holes
- 1¼ yards **large beige floral** for border
- 1⅔ yards **green floral** for outer border
- ⅔ yard **dark green print** for binding
- 4 yards backing fabric
- Quilt batting, at least 72" x 80"
- 5" square of lightweight cardboard for appliqué templates

Center Block
CUTTING

From **beige print**:
Cut one 4½" x 42" strip. From this strip cut two 4½" squares and two 3½" x 4½" rectangles.

Cut one 2½" x 42" strip. From this strip cut one 2½" x 4½" rectangle and twelve 2½" squares.

From **dark green print**:
Cut one 2½" x 42" strip. From this strip cut two 2½" x 8½" rectangles and two 2½" squares.

From **medium green print**:
Cut one 2½" x 42" strip. From this strip cut three 2½" x 8½" rectangles.

From **brown print**:
Cut one 2½" x 42" strip. From this strip cut one 2½" x 4½" rectangle, four 2½" corner squares, and two 1½" squares.

From **blue print #1**:
Cut one 4½" x 8½" rectangle.

From **red print**:
Cut one 2½" x 42" strip.

From **gold print**:
Cut one 2½" x 42" strip.

From **blue print #2**:
Cut two 2½" x 42" strips. From these strips cut four 2½" x 16½" strips.

PIECING
Step 1

Position a 2½" **dark green** square on the corner of the 2½" x 4½" **beige** rectangle. Draw a diagonal line on the square and stitch on the line. Trim the seam allowance to ¼" and press. Repeat this process at the opposite corner of the **beige** rectangle. Sew 2½" **beige** squares to both sides of this unit and press. *At this point the unit should measure 2½" x 8½".*

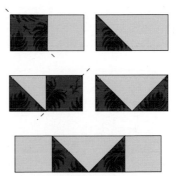

Make 1

Step 2

Position 2½" **beige** squares on the corners of a 2½" x 8½" **dark green** rectangle. Draw a diagonal line on the **beige** squares and stitch on the lines. Trim the seam allowances to ¼" and press.

Make 2

Step 3

Repeat the process in Step 2 using 2½" **beige** squares and a 2½" x 8½" **medium green** rectangle.

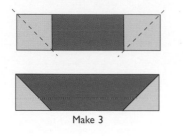

Make 3

Step 4

Position a 1½" **brown** square on the lower right corner of a 3½" x 4½" **beige** rectangle. Draw a diagonal line on the **brown** square and stitch on the line. Trim the seam allowance to ¼" and press. Repeat this process positioning the **brown** square on the lower left corner of the remaining **beige** rectangle.

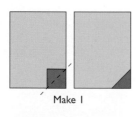

Make 1

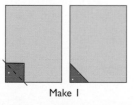

Make 1

Step 5

Sew the Step 4 units to both sides of the 2½" x 4½" **brown** rectangle to complete the trunk unit and press.

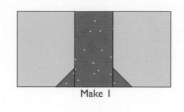

Make 1

Step 6

Sew the Step 1, 2, and 3 units together and press. Add the Step 5 trunk unit to the bottom of this unit and press. *At this point the tree unit should measure 8½" x 16½".*

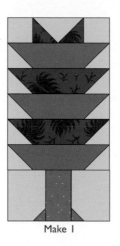

Make 1

Step 7

Position a 4½" **beige** square on the corner of the 4½" x 8½" **blue #1** rectangle. Draw a diagonal line on the **beige** square and stitch on the

line. Trim the seam allowance to ¼" and press. Repeat this process at the opposite corner of the **blue** rectangle. *At this point the roof unit should measure 4½" x 8½".*

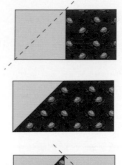

Make 1

Step 8

Aligning long edges, sew the 2½" x 42" **red** and **gold** strips together and press. Cut the strip set into segments. Sew 3 of the segments together end to end and press. Make 4 strips. At this point each strip should measure 2½" x 12½".

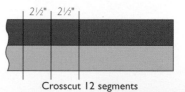

2½"   2½"

Crosscut 12 segments

Make 4

Step 9

Sew the Step 8 strips together, alternating the colors, and press. Sew the Step 7 roof unit to the top of this unit and press. *At this point the house unit should measure 8½" x 16½".*

Make 1

Step 10

Referring to the block diagram, sew the Step 6 tree unit to the left edge of the Step 9 house unit and press.

Step 11

Sew 2½" x 16½" **blue #2** strips to the top and bottom of the house/tree unit and press. Add the 2½" **brown** corner squares to both ends of the remaining 2½" x 16½" **blue** strips and press. Sew these strips to the sides of the unit and

press. *At this point the block should measure 20½" square.*

Appliqué

PREPARE THE BIRDHOUSE HOLE APPLIQUÉS

Step 1

Make cardboard template(s) using the circle pattern.

Step 2

Position the template on the wrong side of the fabric chosen for the appliqué, and trace the template 3 times, leaving a ¾" margin around each shape. Remove the template and cut a scant ¼" beyond the drawn lines.

Step 3

To create smooth, round circles, run a line of basting stitches around each circle, placing the stitches halfway between the drawn line and the cut edge of the circle. After basting, keep the needle and thread attached for the next step.

drawn line

cut edge

template

Make 3
birdhouse holes

Step 4

Place the cardboard template on the wrong side of the fabric circle and tug on the basting stitches, gathering the fabric over the template. When the thread is tight, space the gathers evenly and make a knot to secure the thread. Clip the thread, press the circle, and remove the cardboard template.

Step 5

Appliqué the birdhouse holes to the quilt top.

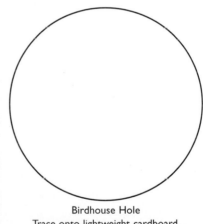

Birdhouse Hole
Trace onto lightweight cardboard.

Borders

NOTE: The yardage given allows for the border strips to be cut on the crosswise grain. Diagonally piece the strips as needed, referring to page 140 for Diagonal Piecing instructions.

CUTTING

From medium green print:

Cut two 7¼" squares. Cut each square diagonally into quarters, forming 8 triangles.

Cut four 2½" x 42" middle border strips.

Cut three 1½" x 42" first inner border strips.

From dark green print:

Cut three 1½" x 42" second inner border strips.

Cut five more 1½" x 42" border strips.

Cut six 2½" x 42" border strips.

From red print:

Cut two 7¼" squares. Cut each square diagonally into quarters, forming 8 triangles.

Cut six 2½" x 42" strips. From these strips cut forty-eight 2½" x 4½" rectangles.

Cut two 2½" x 42" strips.

From beige print:

Cut two 7¼" squares. Cut each square diagonally into quarters, forming 8 triangles.

Cut six 2½" x 42" strips. From these strips cut ninety-six 2½" squares.

From brown print:

Cut one 4½" x 42" strip. From this strip cut four 4½" corner squares.

From gold print:

Cut two 7¼" squares. Cut each square diagonally into quarters, forming 8 triangles.

Cut two 2½" x 42" strips.

From each blue print #1 and blue print #2:

Cut two 7¼" squares. Cut each square diagonally into quarters, forming 8 triangles.

From large beige floral:

Cut six 5½" x 42" border strips.

From green floral:

Cut eight 6½" x 42" outer border strips.

PIECING AND ATTACHING THE BORDERS

Step 1

To attach the 1½"-wide **medium green** first inner border strips to the quilt, refer to page 139 for Border instructions.

Step 2

To attach the 1½"-wide **dark green** second inner border strips to the quilt, refer to page 139 for Border instructions.

Step 3

To make the flying geese units, position a 2½" **beige** square on the corner of a 2½" x 4½" **red** rectangle. Draw a diagonal line on the **beige** square, and stitch on the line. Trim the seam allowance to ¼", and press. Repeat this process at the opposite corner of the **red** rectangle. *At this point the flying geese unit should measure 2½" x 4½".*

Make 48
flying geese units

Step 4

Sew 12 flying geese units together for each side of the quilt and press. *At this point the Flying geese border strip should measure 4½" x 24½".* Sew a flying geese border strip to the top and bottom edge of the quilt and press.

Step 5

Add a 4½" **brown** corner square to both ends of the remaining flying geese border strips, and press. Sew a border strip to each side of the quilt and press. *At this point the quilt center should measure 32½" square.*

Step 6

To attach the 2½"-wide **medium green** middle border strips to the quilt, refer to page 139 for Border instructions.

Step 7

To make the triangle blocks, layer a **beige** triangle on a **blue #1** triangle. Stitch along the bias edge as shown, being careful not to stretch the triangles. Press the seam allowance toward the **blue #1** triangle. Repeat for the remaining **beige** and **blue #1** triangles. Make sure you sew with a **beige** triangle on top, and sew along the same bias edge of each triangle set so your pieced triangle units will all have the **beige** triangles on the same side. Sew the triangle units together in pairs and press. *At this point the block should measure 6½" square.*

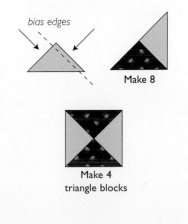

Make 8

Make 4
triangle blocks

Step 8

Repeat Step 7 sewing the **red** and **gold** triangles together to make 4 triangle blocks. Also, sew the **medium green** and **blue #2** triangles together to make 4 triangle blocks.

Make 4
triangle blocks

Make 4
triangle blocks

Step 9

For the top border sew 2 of each coloration of triangle blocks together and press. Repeat this process for the bottom border. *At this point the triangle block border should measure 6½" x 36½".* Sew the borders to the top and bottom of the quilt and press.

Step 10

To make the checkerboard border, align the long edges of the 2½" x 42" **red** and **gold** strips together in pairs, sew and press. Cut the strip sets into segments. For each checkerboard border, sew together 12 segments and press. *At this point the checkerboard border should measure 2½" x 48½".* Sew the strips to the sides of the quilt and press.

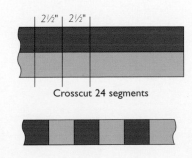

2½" 2½"

Crosscut 24 segments

Step 11

To attach the 1½"-wide **dark green** border strips to the quilt, refer to page 139 for Border instructions.

Step 12

To attach the 5½"-wide **large beige floral** border strips to the quilt, refer to page 139 for Border instructions.

Step 13

To attach the 2½"-wide **dark green** border strips, refer to page 139 for Border instructions.

Step 14

To attach the 6½"-wide **green floral** outer border strips, refer to page 139 for Border instructions.

Putting It All Together

Cut the 4-yard length of backing fabric in half crosswise to make two 2-yard lengths. Refer to Finishing the Quilt on page 139 for complete instructions.

Binding

CUTTING

From **dark green print**:
Cut eight 2¾" x 42" strips.

Sew the binding to the quilt using a ⅜" seam allowance. This measurement will produce a ½"-wide finished double binding. Refer to page 140 for Diagonal Piecing and Binding instructions.

Bird Watching Throw Diagram, 68" x 76"

Double Star
crossing quilt

Double Star crossing quilt

70" x 98"
Block: 14" square (finished)

Fabrics and Supplies

Yardage based on 42"-wide fabric

- 1⅜ yards **gold print** for Eight-Pointed Star blocks and inner border
- 1⅞ yards **beige print** for star blocks and quilt center
- 2¼ yards **red print** for star blocks, quilt center, and checkerboard border
- 1½ yards **chestnut print** for star blocks, quilt center, and checkerboard border
- 2⅞ yards **brown/black plaid** for outer border
- ¾ yard **black print** for binding
- 5¾ yards backing fabric
- Quilt batting, at least 74" x 102"

Eight-Pointed Star Blocks

Make 7 blocks.

CUTTING

From gold print:
Cut two 6½" x 42" strips. From these strips cut seven 6½" squares.

Cut four 2½" x 42" strips. From these strips cut fifty-six 2½" squares.

From beige print:
Cut three 6½" x 42" strips.

Cut seven 2½" x 42" strips. From these strips cut twenty-eight 2½" x 6½" rectangles and twenty-eight 2½" squares.

From red print:
Cut six 2½" x 42" strips.

From chestnut print:
Cut two 2½" x 42" strips. From these strips cut twenty-eight 2½" squares.

PIECING

Step 1

Position 2½" **gold** squares on both corners of a 2½" x 6½" **beige** rectangle. Draw a diagonal line on the **gold** squares and stitch on the lines. Trim the seam allowances to ¼" and press.

Make 28

Step 2

Sew 14 of these units to the top and bottom of the 6½" **gold** squares and press. Sew 2½" **beige** squares to both ends of the remaining 14 Step 1 units and press. Sew the units to the sides of the **gold** square and press. *At this point each star block should measure 10½" square.*

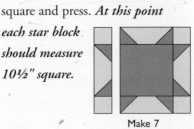

Make 7

Step 3

Sew 2½" x 42" **red print** strips to both sides of a 6½" x 42" **beige** strip and press. Make 3 strip sets. Cut the strip sets into segments. Set aside 10 of the segments to be used to complete the quilt center.

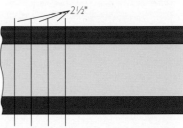

Crosscut 38 segments

Step 4

Sew 14 of the Step 3 segments to the top and bottom of the star blocks and press. Sew 2½" **chestnut print** squares to both ends of 14 of the Step 3 segments and press. Sew the units to the sides of the star blocks and press. *At this point each star block should measure 14½" square.*

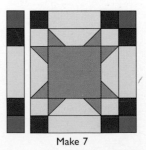

Make 7

Four-Pointed Star Blocks

Make 8 blocks.

CUTTING

From beige print:

Cut four 2½" x 42" strips. From these strips cut sixteen 2½" x 4½" rectangles and thirty-two 2½" squares.

Cut two more 2½" x 42" strips.

From red print:

Cut three 2½" x 42" strips. From these strips cut eight 2½" x 6½" rectangles and sixteen 2½" squares.

Cut ten 2½" x 42" strips.

From chestnut print:

Cut eight 2½" x 42" strips.

PIECING

Step 1

Position 2½" **beige** squares on both corners of a 2½" x 6½" **red** rectangle. Draw a diagonal line on the **beige** squares and stitch on the lines. Trim the seam allowances to ¼" and press.

Make 8

Step 2

Position a 2½" **red** square on the right corner of a 2½" x 4½" **beige** rectangle. Draw a diagonal line on the **red** square and stitch on the line. Trim the seam allowance to ¼" and press. Add a 2½" **beige** square to the right edge and press.

Make 16

Step 3

Sew Step 2 units to both sides of the Step 1 units and press. *At this point each star block should measure 6½" square.*

Make 8

Step 4

Aligning long edges, sew together the eight 2½" x 42" **chestnut print** strips and 8 of the 2½" x 42" **red** strips in pairs and press. Make 8 strip sets. Cut the strip sets into segments.

Crosscut 128 segments

Step 5

Aligning long edges, sew together 2 of the 2½" x 42" **beige** strips and 2 of the 2½" x 42" **red** strips in pairs and press. Make 2 strip sets. Cut the strip sets into segments.

Crosscut 32 segments

Step 6

Sew Step 4 segments to both sides of 16 of the Step 5 segments and press. Referring to the Step 8 block diagram, sew the units to the top and bottom of the star blocks and press. The remaining 16 Step 5 units will be used in Step 7.

Make 16

Step 7

Sew 3 of the Step 4 units together and press. Make 32 units. Sew the units to both sides of the remaining Step 5 units and press.

Make 32

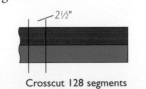

Make 16

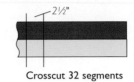

Step 8

Referring to the block diagram, sew the Step 7 units to both sides of the star blocks and press. *At this point each star block should measure 14½" square.*

Make 8

Quilt Center

CUTTING

From **chestnut print**:
Cut four 2½" x 42" strips.

From **red print**:
Cut four 2½" x 42" strips.

Cut one more 2½" x 42" strip. From this strip cut six 2½" squares.

From **beige print**:
Cut three 2½" x 42" strips. From these strips cut ten 2½" x 10½" rectangles and six 2½" squares.

QUILT CENTER ASSEMBLY

Step 1

Aligning long edges, sew together the 2½" x 42" **chestnut print** strips and the 2½" x 42" **red** strips in pairs and press. Make 4 strip sets. Cut the strip sets into segments.

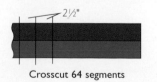

2½"

Crosscut 64 segments

Step 2

Sew 4 of the Step 1 segments together and press. Make 6 of Unit A and 6 of Unit B.

Unit A, Make 6   Unit B, Make 6

Step 3

Sew 3 of the Step 1 segments together and press. Make 4 of Unit C.

Unit C, Make 4

Step 4

Sew together the 2½" **beige** and **red** squares in pairs and press.

Make 6

Step 5

Sew a 2½" x 10½" **beige** rectangle to the bottom of a remaining Step 3 segment from the eight-point star section and press.

Make 10

Step 6

For the top and bottom quilt center strips, sew together 2 of the Step 1 segments, 1 of the Step 2 A Units, 1 of the Step 2 B Units, 1 of the Step 4 segments, and 2 of the Step 5 units and press.

At this point each strip should measure 4½" x 42½". Make 2.

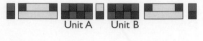

Unit A   Unit B

Step 7

For each side quilt center strip, sew together 2 of the Step 2 A Units, 2 of the Step 2 B Units, 2 of the Step 3 C Units, 2 of the Step 4 units, and 3 of the Step 5 units and press. *At this point each strip should measure 4½" x 78½".* Make 2.

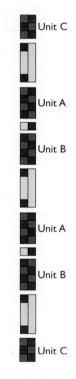

Unit C

Unit A

Unit B

Unit A

Unit B

Unit C

Step 8

Referring to the quilt diagram, sew together the Eight-Pointed Star blocks and the Four-Pointed Star blocks in 5 horizontal rows of 3 blocks each. Press the seam allowances in alternating directions by rows so they will fit together snugly.

Step 9

Pin the rows together at the block intersections, and stitch. Press the seam allowances in one direction. *At this point the quilt center should measure 42½" x 70½".*

Step 10

Referring to the quilt diagram, sew the Step 6 quilt center top/bottom strips to the quilt center and press.

Step 11

Referring to the quilt diagram, sew the Step 7 quilt center side strips to the quilt center and press. *At this point the quilt center should measure 50½" x 78½".*

Borders

NOTE: The yardage given allows for the inner border and checkerboard border strips to be cut on the crosswise grain. Diagonally piece the strips together as needed, referring to page 140 for Diagonal Piecing instructions. The yardage given allows for the outer border strips to be cut on the lengthwise grain. Cutting the strips on the lengthwise grain will eliminate the need for piecing and matching the plaid outer border strips.

CUTTING

From gold print:
Cut seven 2½" x 42" inner border strips.

From chestnut print:
Cut five 2½" x 42" strips for checkerboard border.

From red print:
Cut five 2½" x 42" strips for checkerboard border.

From brown/black plaid (cut on the lengthwise grain):
Cut two 6½" x 100" side outer border strips.
Cut two 6½" x 60" top/bottom outer border strips.

ATTACHING THE BORDERS

Step 1

To attach the 2½"-wide **gold** inner border strips, refer to page 139 for Border instructions.

Step 2

To make the checkerboard border, sew together a 2½" x 42" **chestnut** strip and a 2½" x 42" **red** strip and press. Make 5 strip sets. Cut the strip sets into segments.

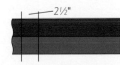

Crosscut 72 segments

Step 3

For the top and bottom checkerboard borders, sew together 14 of the Step 2 segments and press. Remove one **red** square from the end of each strip and press. Sew the border strips to the quilt and press.

Step 4

For the side checkerboard borders, sew together 22 of the Step 2 segments and press. Remove one **chestnut** square from each strip and press. Sew the border strips to the quilt and press.

Step 5

To attach the 6½"-wide **brown/black plaid** outer border strips, refer to page 139 for Border instructions.

Putting It All Together

Cut the 5¾-yard length of backing fabric in half crosswise to make two 2⅞-yard lengths. Refer to Finishing the Quilt on page 139 for complete instructions.

Binding

CUTTING

From black print:
Cut nine 2¾" x 42" strips.

Sew the binding to the quilt using a ⅜" seam allowance. This measurement will produce a ½"-wide finished double binding. Refer to page 140 for Diagonal Piecing and Binding instructions.

Double Star Crossing Quilt Diagram, 70" x 98"

Fall Colors
table runner

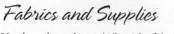

Fall Colors table runner
30" x 40"

Fabrics and Supplies

Yardage based on 42"-wide fabric

- ⅓ yard **beige print** for center panel
- ¼ yard **dark red print** for center panel
- ⅛ yard **red print** for center panel
- Ten 8½" squares of **assorted prints** for triangle blocks*
- ¼ yard **black print** for inner border
- ⅝ yard **green floral** for outer border
- ⅜ yard **black print** for binding
- 1¼ yards backing fabric
- Quilt batting, at least 34" x 44"

*We used six 8½" x 17" assorted prints and cut two 8½" squares from each print.

Center Panel

CUTTING

From **beige print**:
Cut one 8½" x 18½" rectangle.

Cut four 4½" squares.

From **dark red print**:
Cut two 4½" x 8½" rectangles.

From **red print**:
Cut two 2½" x 8½" rectangles.

PIECING

Step 1

Position a 4½" **beige** square on the corner of a 4½" x 8½" **dark red** rectangle. Draw a diagonal line on the **beige** square and stitch on the line. Trim the seam allowance to ¼" and press. Repeat this process at the opposite corner of the **dark red** rectangle.

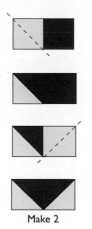

Make 2

Step 2

Sew the Step 1 units to both ends of the 8½" x 18½" **beige** rectangle and press.

Step 3

Add the 2½" x 8½" **red** rectangles to both ends of the center unit and press. *At this point the center panel should measure 8½" x 30½".*

Triangle Blocks

Make 10 blocks.

CUTTING

From the 10 **assorted prints***:
Cut a total of ten 7¼" squares. Cut the squares diagonally into quarters to make 40 triangles.

*We cut a total of twelve 7¼" squares from 6 assorted prints, cutting the squares diagonally into quarters to make 48 triangles. You will only use 40 triangles.

PIECING

Step 1

Layer a **dark** triangle on a **light** triangle. Stitch along the bias edge as shown, being careful not to stretch the triangles. Press the seam allowance toward the **dark** triangle. Repeat for the remaining triangles, stitching along the same bias edge of each triangle set. Sew the triangle units together in pairs and press. *At this point each triangle block should measure 6½" square.*

bias edges

Make 20 triangle units

Make 10 triangle blocks

Step 2

Sew 5 of the triangle blocks together and press. *At this point each strip should measure 6½" x 30½".*

Make 2

Step 3

Sew the Step 2 strips to both sides of the runner center panel and press.

Borders

NOTE: The yardage given allows for the borders to be cut on the crosswise grain. Diagonally piece the strips as needed, referring to page 140 for Diagonal Piecing instructions.

CUTTING

From **black print**:
Cut three 1½" x 42" inner border strips.

From **green floral**:
Cut four 4½" x 42" outer border strips.

ATTACHING THE BORDERS

Step 1

To attach the 1½"-wide **black** inner border strips, refer to page 139 for Border instructions.

Step 2

To attach the 4½"-wide **green floral** outer border strips, refer to page 139 for Border instructions.

Putting It All Together

Trim the batting and backing so they are 4" larger than the quilt top. Refer to Finishing the Quilt on page 139 for complete instructions.

Binding

CUTTING

From **black print**:
Cut four 2¾" x 42" strips.

Sew the binding to the quilt using a ⅜" seam allowance. This measurement will produce a ½"-wide finished double binding. Refer to page 140 for Diagonal Piecing and Binding instructions.

Fall Colors Table Runner Diagram, 30" x 40"

Flower Block
wall quilt

Flower Block wall quilt

60" square
Block: 16" square (finished)

Fabrics and Supplies

Yardage based on 42"-wide fabric

- 1 yard **beige print** for background and lattice strips
- ⅛ yard **coral print #1** for flower center
- ½ yard **coral print #2** for flower center and fence
- ½ yard **eggplant print #1** for flower and corner square
- 1 yard **light green print** for inner leaves and fence background
- ¾ yard **dark green print** for outer leaves and center square
- ⅜ yard **brick print** for fence
- ⅓ yard **eggplant print #2** for inner border
- ⅓ yard **gold print** for first middle border
- ⅓ yard **red print** for second middle border
- 1¾ yards **large beige floral** for outer border
- ⅝ yard **dark green print** for binding
- 3¾ yards backing fabric
- Quilt batting, at least 64" square

Flower Block

Make 4 blocks.

CUTTING

From **beige print**:
Cut five 2⅞" x 42" strips.

Cut four 2½" x 42" strips. From these strips cut sixty-four 2½" squares.

From **coral print #1**:
Cut one 2½" x 42" strip. From this strip cut eight 2½" squares.

From **coral print #2**:
Cut one 2½" x 42" strip. From this strip cut eight 2½" squares.

From **eggplant print #1**:
Cut three 2½" x 42" strips. From these strips cut sixteen 2½" x 4½" rectangles and sixteen 2½" squares.

Cut one 1½" x 42" strip. From this strip cut sixteen 1½" squares.

From **light green print**:
Cut two 2⅞" x 42" strips.

Cut three 2½" x 42" strips. From these strips cut sixteen 2½" x 4½" rectangles and sixteen 2½" squares.

Cut two 1½" x 42" strips. From these strips cut thirty-two 1½" squares.

From **dark green print**:
Cut three 2⅞" x 42" strips.

Cut three 2½" x 42" strips. From these strips cut sixteen 2½" x 4½" rectangles and sixteen 2½" squares.

PIECING

Step 1

Position a 1½" **eggplant** square on the upper left corner of a 2½" **coral #1** square. Draw a diagonal line on the **eggplant** square and stitch on the line. Trim the seam allowance to ¼" and press.

Make 8

Step 2

Position a 1½" **eggplant** square on the upper right corner of a 2½" **coral #2** square. Draw a diagonal line on the **eggplant** square and stitch on the line. Trim the seam allowance to ¼" and press.

Make 8

Step 3

Sew the Step 1 and Step 2 units together in pairs and press. Sew the pairs together and press. *At this point each flower center should measure 4½" square.*

Make 4

Step 4

Position a 1½" **light green** square on the corner of a 2½" **eggplant** square. Draw a diagonal line on the **green** square and stitch on the line. Trim the seam allowance to ¼" and press. Make 16. Sew the units together in pairs and press. Sew the pairs to the top and bottom of the Step 3 flower center and press.

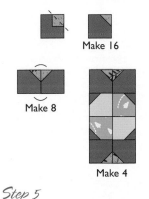

Make 16

Make 8

Make 4

Step 5

Position a 1½" **light green** square on the upper right corner of a 2½" x 4½" **eggplant** rectangle. Draw a diagonal line on the **green** square and stitch on the line. Trim the seam allowance to ¼" and press.

Make 8

Step 6

Position a 1½" **light green** square on the upper left corner of a 2½" x 4½" **eggplant** rectangle. Draw a diagonal line on the square, stitch, trim, and press.

Make 8

Step 7

Sew the Step 5 and Step 6 units together in pairs and press. *At this point each unit should measure 2½" x 8½".*

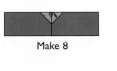

Make 8

Step 8

Sew the Step 7 units to the sides of the Step 4 flower center and press. *At this point each flower should measure 8½" square.*

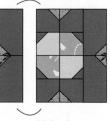

Make 4

Step 9

Position a 2½" **beige** square on the corner of a 2½" x 4½" **light green** rectangle. Draw a diagonal line on the **beige** square and stitch on the line. Trim the seam allowance to ¼" and press. Repeat this process at the opposite corner of the **light green** rectangle. *At this point each unit should measure 2½" x 4½".*

Make 16

Step 10

Repeat Step 9 using 2½" **beige** squares and 2½" x 4½" **dark green** rectangles.

Make 16

Step 11

With right sides together, layer the 2⅞" x 42" **light green** strips and 2 of the **beige** strips in pairs. Press together, but do not sew. Cut the layered strips into squares. Cut the layered squares in half diagonally to make 32 sets of triangles. Stitch ¼" from the diagonal edge of each pair of triangles and press. *At this point each triangle-pieced square should measure 2½" square.*

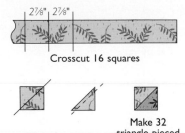

Crosscut 16 squares

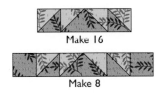

Make 32
triangle-pieced
2½" squares

Step 12

Referring to the diagram, sew Step 11 triangle-pieced squares to both sides of the Step 9 units and press. Sew a unit to the top and bottom of each Step 8 flower unit and press. Add a 2½" **light green** square to both ends of the remaining units and press. Referring to the block diagram, sew the units to the sides of the flower/leaf unit and press. *At this point each flower/leaf unit should measure 12½" square.*

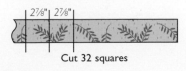

Make 16

Make 8

Step 13

With right sides together, layer the 2⅞" x 42" **dark green** strips and 3 of the **beige** strips in pairs. Press together, but do not sew. Cut the layered strips into squares. Cut the squares in half diagonally to make 64 sets of triangles. Stitch ¼" from the diagonal edge of each pair of triangles and press. *At this point each triangle-pieced square should measure 2½" square.*

Cut 32 squares

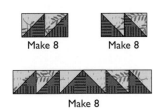

Make 64
triangle-pieced
2½" squares

Step 14

Sew the Step 13 triangle-pieced squares together in pairs and press. Sew the pairs to both sides of the Step 10 units and press. *At this point each unit should measure 2½" x 12½".*

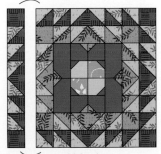

Make 8   Make 8

Make 8

Step 15

Referring to the block diagram, sew Step 14 units to the top and bottom of Step 12 flower/leaf unit and press. Add 2½" **dark green** squares to both ends of the remaining Step 14 units and press. Sew the units to the sides of the flower/leaf unit and press. *At this point each block should measure 16½" square.*

Make 4

Quilt Center

CUTTING

From **beige print**:
Cut two 4½" x 42" strips. From

these strips cut four 4½" x 16½" lattice strips.

From **dark green print**:
Cut one 4½" center square.

From **coral print #2**:
Cut four 2½" x 42" strips. From these strips cut thirty-six 2½" x 4½" rectangles.

From **brick print**:
Cut four 2½" x 42" strips. From these strips cut thirty-six 2½" x 4½" rectangles.

From **light green print**:
Cut five 2½" x 42" strips. From these strips cut seventy-two 2½" squares.

From **eggplant print #1**:
Cut one 4½" x 42" strip. From this strip cut four 4½" corner squares.

QUILT CENTER ASSEMBLY

Step 1

Sew a flower block to both sides of a 4½" x 16½" **beige** lattice strip. Press the seam allowances toward the lattice strip. *At this point each block row should measure 16½" x 36½".*

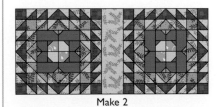

Make 2

Step 2

Sew a 4½" x 16½" **beige** lattice strip to both sides of the 4½" **dark green** square. Press the seam allowances toward the lattice strips.

At this point the lattice strip should measure 4½" x 36½".

Make 1

Step 3

Sew the block rows to the top and bottom of the lattice strip and press.

Step 4

Position a 2½" **light green** square on the corner of a 2½" x 4½" **brick** rectangle. Draw a diagonal line on the **green** square and stitch on the line. Trim the seam allowance to ¼" and press.

Make 36

Step 5

Repeat the Step 4 process using a 2½" **light green** square and a 2½" x 4½" **coral #2** rectangle. Be sure to reverse the direction of the drawn sewing line.

Make 36

Step 6

Sew the Step 4 and Step 5 units together in pairs and press.

Make 36
fence units

Step 7

For the fence borders, sew together 9 of the Step 6 fence units and press. *At this point each fence border should measure 4½" x 36½".* Sew the fence borders to the top and bottom of the quilt center and press.

Make 4

Step 8

Sew a 4½" **eggplant** corner square to both ends of the remaining fence borders and press. *At this point each fence border should measure 4½" x 44½".* Sew the strips to the sides of the quilt center and press.

Borders

NOTE: The yardage given allows for the 3 narrow border strips to be cut on the crosswise grain. Diagonally piece the strips as needed, referring to page 140 for Diagonal Piecing instructions. The yardage given for the **large beige floral** outer border strips allows for these strips to be cut on the lengthwise grain.

CUTTING

From **eggplant print #2:**
Cut five 1½" x 42" border strips.

From **gold print:**
Cut five 1½" x 42" first middle border strips.

From **red print:**
Cut six 1½" x 42" second middle border strips.

From **large beige floral** (cut on the lengthwise grain):
Cut four 5½" x 63" outer border strips.

ATTACHING THE BORDERS

Step 1

To attach the 1½"-wide **eggplant #2** inner border strips, refer to page 139 for Border instructions.

Step 2

To attach the 1½"-wide **gold** first middle border strips, refer to page 139 for Border instructions.

Step 3

To attach the 1½"-wide **red** second middle border strips, refer to page 139 for Border instructions.

Step 4

To attach the 5½"-wide **large beige floral** outer border strips, refer to page 139 for Border instructions.

Putting It All Together

Cut the 3¾-yard length of backing fabric in half crosswise to make two 1⅞-yard lengths. Refer to Finishing the Quilt on page 139 for complete instructions.

Binding

CUTTING

From dark green print:
Cut seven 2¾" x 42" strips.

Sew the binding to the quilt using a ⅜" seam allowance. This measurement will produce a ½"-wide finished double binding. Refer to page 140 for Diagonal Piecing and Binding instructions.

Flower Block Wall Quilt Diagram, 60" square

Cell phones and palm pilots,

carpools and computers…how

did life become so busy? Time

to slip away to a special place,

snuggle up in your favorite

quilt, and treat yourself to a

gentle repose.

Retreat

Use your *Quiet time*
to do something you love:
make a quilt!

"What better way to *renew* your physical and spiritual self, to *recharge* your batteries, than to retreat to a *secret* "nest"..."

Bear Paw
scramble

Bear Paw scramble

82" x 98"
Block: 8" square (finished)

Fabrics and Supplies

Yardage based on 42"-wide fabric

- 1½ yards **beige/green print** for pieced blocks
- 2 yards **green print** for pieced blocks and second middle border
- 2⅛ yards **beige print** for pieced blocks
- 1⅔ yards **black print #1** for pieced blocks
- ½ yard **chestnut print** for inner border
- ½ yard **black print #2** for first middle border
- 2 yards **green floral** for outer border
- ⅞ yard **black print #2** for binding
- 7⅛ yards backing fabric
- Quilt batting, at least 86" x 102"

Pieced Blocks

Make 80 blocks.

CUTTING

From **beige/green print:**
Cut seven 6⅞" x 42" strips.

From **green print:**
Cut seven 6⅞" x 42" strips.

From **beige print:**
Cut eighteen 2⅞" x 42" strips.

Cut five 2½" x 42" strips. From these strips cut eighty 2½" squares.

From **black print #1:**
Cut eighteen 2⅞" x 42" strips.

PIECING

Step 1

With right sides together, layer the 6⅞" x 42" **beige/green print** and **green print** strips in pairs. Press together, but do not sew. Cut the layered strips into squares. Cut the layered squares in half diagonally to make 80 sets of triangles. Stitch ¼" from the diagonal edge of each pair of triangles and press. *At this point each triangle-pieced square should measure 6½" square.*

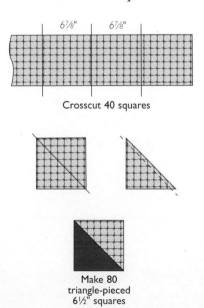

Crosscut 40 squares

Make 80
triangle-pieced
6½" squares

Step 2

With right sides together, layer the 2⅞" x 42" **beige** and **black print #1** strips in pairs. Press together, but do not sew. Cut the layered strips into squares. Cut the layered squares in half diagonally to make 480 sets of triangles. Stitch ¼" from the diagonal edge of each pair of triangles and press. *At this point each triangle-pieced square should measure 2½" square.*

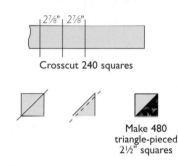

Crosscut 240 squares

Make 480
triangle-pieced
2½" squares

Step 3

Sew 3 of the Step 2 triangle-pieced squares together and press. Make 80 units. Sew each of the units to the top edge of the Step 1 triangle-pieced squares. *At this point each unit should measure 6½" x 8½".*

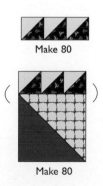

Make 80

( )

Make 80

Step 4

Sew 3 of the Step 2 triangle-pieced squares together and press. Add a 2½" **beige** square to the left edge of this unit and press. Make 80 units. Sew each of the units to the right edge of the Step 3 units and press. *At this point each block should measure 8½" square.*

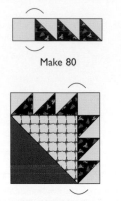

Make 80

Make 80

Quilt Center

Step 1

Referring to the quilt diagram for block placement, sew the pieced blocks together in 10 horizontal rows of 8 blocks each. Press the seam allowances in alternating directions by rows so the seams will fit snugly together with less bulk.

Step 2

Pin the rows together at the block intersections and sew the rows together. Press the seam allowances in one direction. *At this point the quilt center should measure 64½" x 80½".*

Borders

NOTE: The yardage given allows for the border strips to be cut on the crosswise grain. Diagonally piece the strips as needed, referring to page 140 for Diagonal Piecing instructions.

CUTTING

From **chestnut print**:
Cut eight 1½" x 42" inner border strips.

From **black print #2**:
Cut eight 1½" x 42" first middle border strips.

From **green print**:
Cut eight 1½" x 42" second middle border strips.

From **green floral**:
Cut ten 6½" x 42" outer border strips.

ATTACHING THE BORDERS

Step 1

To attach the 1½"-wide **chestnut** inner border strips, refer to page 139 for Border instructions.

Step 2

To attach the 1½"-wide **black print #2** first middle border strips, refer to page 139 for Border instructions.

Step 3

To attach the 1½"-wide **green print** second middle border strips, refer to page 139 for Border instructions.

Step 4

To attach the 6½"-wide **green floral** outer border strips, refer to page 139 for Border instructions.

Putting It All Together

Cut the 7⅛-yard length of backing fabric in thirds crosswise to make three 2⅜-yard lengths. Refer to Finishing the Quilt on page 139 for complete instructions.

Binding

CUTTING

From **black print #2**:
Cut ten 2¾" x 42" strips.

Sew the binding to the quilt using a ⅜" seam allowance. This measurement will produce a ½"-wide finished double binding. Refer to page 140 for Diagonal Piecing and Binding instructions.

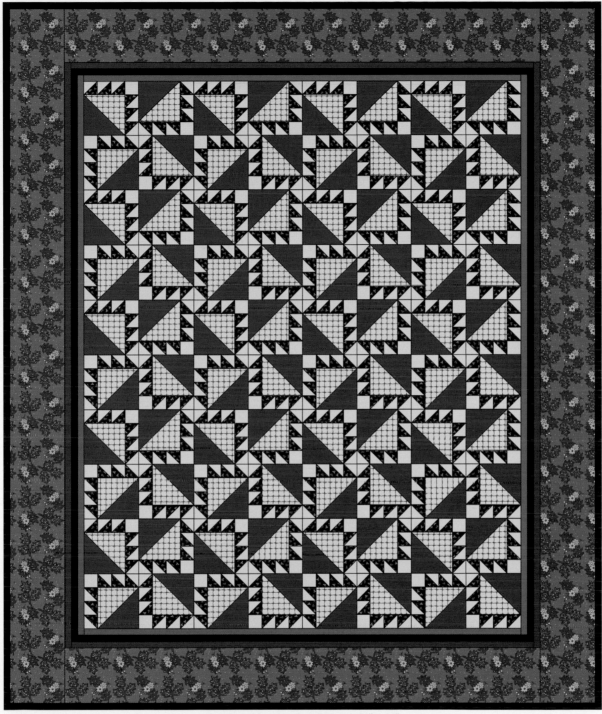

Bear Paw Scramble Quilt Diagram, 82" x 98"

Bed Roll
76" x 96" **snugly**

Fabrics and Supplies

Yardage based on 42"-wide fabric

- ¾ yard **green floral** for top section
- ⅓ yard **red print** for middle band
- 4½ yards **green print** for lower section
- 2¼ yards **green plaid** for bias binding
- 5½ yards backing fabric
- Quilt batting, at least 80" x 100"

CUTTING

From green floral:

Cut two 12½" x 42" strips. Remove the selvages, sew the short ends together and press. Trim the strip to 12½" x 76".

From red print:

Cut two 3½" x 42" strips. Remove the selvages, sew the short ends together and press. Trim the strip to 3½" x 76".

From green print:

Cut the 4½ yard length in half crosswise to make two 2¼ yard lengths. Remove the selvages, sew the long edges together and press. Trim to 76" x 81".

PIECING

Step 1

Aligning long edges, sew the 3½" x 76" **red** strip to the 12½" x 76" **green floral** strip and press.

Step 2

Aligning edges, sew the Step 1 unit to the 76" x 81" **green** rectangle and press. *At this point the quilt top should measure 76" x 96".*

Putting It All Together

Cut the 5½-yard length of backing fabric in half crosswise to make two 2¾-yard lengths. Refer to Finishing the Quilt on page 139 for complete instructions.

Binding

CUTTING

From green plaid:

Cut enough 6½"-wide bias strips to make a 360"-long strip.

Sew the binding to the quilt using a scant 1" seam allowance. This measurement will produce a 1"-wide finished double binding. Refer to page 140 for Diagonal Piecing and Binding instructions.

Bed Roll Snugly Diagram, 76" x 96"

red Rhapsody

67" square

Block: 12" square (finished)

Fabrics and Supplies

Yardage based on 42"-wide fabric

- ⅝ yard **red print #1** for pieced blocks
- 1⅛ yards **green print** for pieced blocks and inner border
- 2½ yards **beige print** for pieced blocks, alternate blocks, and side and corner triangles
- ⅓ yard **green check** for pieced blocks
- 1⅓ yards **red print #2** for outer border
- ⅔ yard **green print** for binding
- 4 yards backing fabric
- Quilt batting, at least 71" square

Pieced Blocks

Make 9 blocks.

CUTTING

From **red print #1**:

Cut two 4½" x 42" strips. From these strips cut nine 4½" squares.

Cut three 2½" x 42" strips. From these strips cut thirty-six 2½" squares.

From **green print**:

Cut seven 2½" x 42" strips. From these strips cut thirty-six 2½" x 4½" rectangles and thirty-six 2½" squares.

From **beige print**:

Cut three 2⅞" x 42" strips.

Cut nine 2½" x 42" strips. From these strips cut thirty-six 2½" x 4½" rectangles and seventy-two 2½" squares.

From **green check**:

Cut three 2⅞" x 42" strips.

PIECING

Step 1

Position a 2½" **beige** square on the corner of a 2½" x 4½" **green** rectangle. Draw a diagonal line on the **beige** square and stitch on the line. Trim the seam allowance to ¼" and press. Repeat this process at the opposite corner of the **green** rectangle. *At this point each unit should measure 2½" x 4½".*

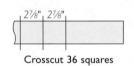

Make 36

Step 2

Sew a 2½" x 4½" **beige** rectangle to the top of each of the Step 1 units and press. *At this point each unit should measure 4½" square.*

Make 36

Step 3

With right sides together, layer the 2⅞" x 42" **beige** and **green check** strips in pairs. Press together, but do not sew. Cut the layered strips into squares. Cut the layered squares in half diagonally to make 72 sets of triangles. Stitch ¼" from the diagonal edge of each pair of triangles and press. *At this point each triangle-pieced square should measure 2½" square.*

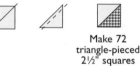

Crosscut 36 squares

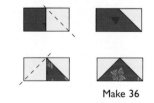

Make 72 triangle-pieced 2½" squares

Step 4

Referring to the diagrams, sew 36 of the triangle-pieced squares to the 2½" **red #1** squares. Press the seam allowances toward the **red #1** squares. Sew 36 of the triangle-pieced squares to the 2½" **green** squares. Press the seam allowances toward the **green** squares. Sew the units together in pairs and press. *At this point each unit should measure 4½" square.*

Make 36   Make 36

Make 36

Step 5

Referring to the block diagram, sew the Step 2 units to the top and bottom of the 4½" red #1 squares and press. Sew the Step 4 units to both ends of the remaining Step 2 units and press. Sew the units together and press. *At this point each block should measure 12½" square.*

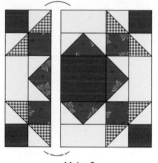

Make 9

Quilt Center

NOTE: The side and corner triangles are larger than necessary and will be trimmed before the borders are added.

CUTTING

From **beige print**:

Cut one 19" x 42" strip. From this strip cut two 19" squares. Cut the squares diagonally into quarters for a total of 8 side triangles.

Cut two 12½" x 42" strips. From these strips cut four 12½" alternate blocks and two 10" squares. Cut the squares in half diagonally for a total of 4 corner triangles.

QUILT CENTER ASSEMBLY

Step 1

Referring to the quilt diagram for block placement, sew the pieced blocks, alternate blocks, and side triangles together in 5 diagonal rows. Press the seam allowances toward the alternate blocks and side triangles.

Step 2

Pin the rows together at the block intersections and stitch. Press the seam allowances in one direction.

Step 3

Sew the corner triangles to the quilt center and press.

Step 4

Trim away the excess fabric from the side and corner triangles taking care to allow a ¼" seam allowance beyond the corners of each block. Refer to Trimming Side and Corner Triangles on page 140 for complete instructions.

Borders

NOTE: The yardage given allows for the border strips to be cut on the crosswise grain. Diagonally piece the strips as needed, referring to page 140 for Diagonal Piecing instructions.

CUTTING

From **green print**:

Cut six 2½" x 42" inner border strips.

From **red print #2**:

Cut seven 6½" x 42" outer border strips.

ATTACHING THE BORDERS

Step 1

To attach the 2½"-wide **green** inner border strips, refer to page 139 for Border instructions.

Step 2

To attach the 6½"-wide **red #2** outer border strips, refer to page 139 for Border instructions.

Putting It All Together

Cut the 4-yard length of backing fabric in half crosswise to make two 2-yard lengths. Refer to Finishing the Quilt on page 139 for complete instructions.

Binding

CUTTING

From **green print**:

Cut seven 2¾" x 42" strips.

Sew the binding to the quilt using a ⅜" seam allowance. This measurement will produce a ½"-wide finished double binding. Refer to page 140 for Diagonal Piecing and Binding instructions.

Red Rhapsody Quilt Diagram, 67" square

Star Garland *54" square* table topper

Fabrics and Supplies

Yardage is based on 42"-wide fabric

- 1⅝ yards **red print #1** for checkerboard center, outer border and "ribbon" appliqués
- ½ yard **beige print** for checkerboard center
- ⅞ yard **green print #1** for wide inner border
- ¼ yard **tan print** for Nine-Patch corner squares
- ¼ yard **red/green print** for Nine-Patch corner squares
- ¼ yard **red floral** for narrow inner border
- 1 yard **green print #2** for middle border and binding
- ⅓ yard **red print #2** for "ribbon" appliqués
- ½ yard **gold print #1** for large star appliqués
- ¼ yard **gold print #2** for small star appliqués
- 3¼ yards backing fabric
- 2 yards paper-backed fusible web for appliqués
- Template material for appliqués
- Matching thread for appliqués
- Quilt batting, at least 58" square

Checkerboard Center

CUTTING

From **red print #1**:
Cut three 4½" x 42" strips.

From **beige print**:
Cut three 4½" x 42" strips.

PIECING

Step 1

Aligning long edges, sew the 4½" x 42" **red #1** and **beige** strips together in pairs. Press the seam allowances toward the **red** fabric referring to Hints and Helps for Pressing Strip Sets. Make 3 strip sets. Cut the strip sets into segments.

4½" | 4½"

Crosscut 25 segments

Step 2

Sew 7 of the segments together side by side and press. Make 3 of these strips. Sew the strips together and press. Sew 4 of the segments together end to end. Remove the **beige** square from one end and press. Sew this strip to the checkerboard unit and press.

At this point the checkerboard center should measure 28½" square.

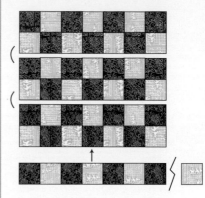

Borders and Nine-Patch Corner Squares

NOTE: The yardage given allows for the border strips to be cut on the crosswise grain. Diagonally piece the strips as needed, referring to page 140 for Diagonal Piecing instructions.

CUTTING

From **green print #1**:
Cut four 6½" x 42" inner border strips.

From **red/green print**:
Cut one 2½" x 42" strip for Nine-Patch corner squares.

Cut two 2½" x 20" strips for Nine-Patch corner squares.

From **tan print**:

Cut two 2½" x 42" strips for Nine-Patch corner squares.

Cut one 2½" x 20" strip for Nine-Patch corner squares.

From **red floral**:

Cut four 1½" x 42" narrow inner border strips.

From **green print #2**:

Cut five 2½" x 42" middle border strips.

From **red print #1**:

Cut six 4½" x 42" outer border strips.

PIECING THE NINE-PATCH CORNER SQUARES

Step 1

Aligning long edges, sew a 2½" x 42" **tan** strip to both sides of a 2½" x 42" **red/green** strip and press. Cut the strip set into segments.

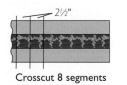

Crosscut 8 segments

Step 2

Aligning long edges, sew a 2½" x 20" **red/green** strip to both sides of a 2½" x 20" **tan** strip and press. Cut the strip into segments.

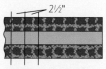

Crosscut 4 segments

Step 3

To make the Nine-Patch corner square, sew a Step 1 segment to both sides of a Step 2 segment and press. ***At this point each Nine-Patch corner square should measure 6½" square.***

Make 4 Nine-Patch corner squares

ATTACHING THE BORDERS

Step 1

To attach the 6½"-wide **green #1** top and bottom inner border strips, refer to page 139 for Border instructions.

Step 2

To attach the 6½"-wide **green #1** side inner border strips with Nine-Patch corner squares, refer to page 139 for Borders with Corner Squares.

Step 3

To attach the 1½"-wide **red floral** narrow inner border strips, refer to page 139 for Border instructions.

Step 4

To attach the 2½"-wide **green #2** middle border strips, refer to page 139 for Border instructions.

Step 5

To attach the 4½"-wide **red #1** outer border strips, refer to page 139 for Border instructions.

Fusible Web Appliqué

Step 1

Make templates using the appliqué patterns on pages 81-82.

Step 2

Position the templates on the fusible web, paper side up, making sure the shapes are at least ½" apart. With a pencil, trace the shapes the number of times indicated on each pattern. Cut the shapes apart leaving a small margin beyond the drawn lines.

NOTE: When you are fusing a large shape like the large star, fuse just the outer edges of the shape so that it will not look stiff when finished. To do this, draw a line about ⅜" inside the shape and cut away the fusible web on this line.

Step 3

Following the manufacturer's instructions, fuse the shapes to the wrong side of the fabrics chosen for the appliqués. Let the fabric cool and cut along the traced line of each shape. Peel away the paper backing.

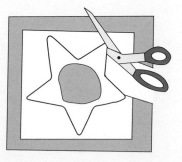

Step 4

Referring to the table topper diagram, position the "ribbon" appliqués on the topper and pin in place. The B "ribbon" will overlap the tip of the A "ribbon" about ½". With a hot, dry iron, fuse the shapes in place. With matching thread, machine-zigzag stitch the "ribbon" appliqués. Position the stars on the table topper as dia-gramed and fuse in place. With matching thread, machine-zigzag the star appliqués.

Putting It All Together

Cut the 3¼-yard length of backing fabric in half crosswise to make two 1⅝-yard lengths. Refer to Finishing the Quilt on page 139 for complete instructions.

Binding

CUTTING

From **green print #2**:
Cut six 2¾" x 42" strips.

Sew the binding to the quilt using a ⅜" seam allowance. This measurement will produce a ½"-wide finished double binding. Refer to page 140 for Diagonal Piecing and Binding instructions.

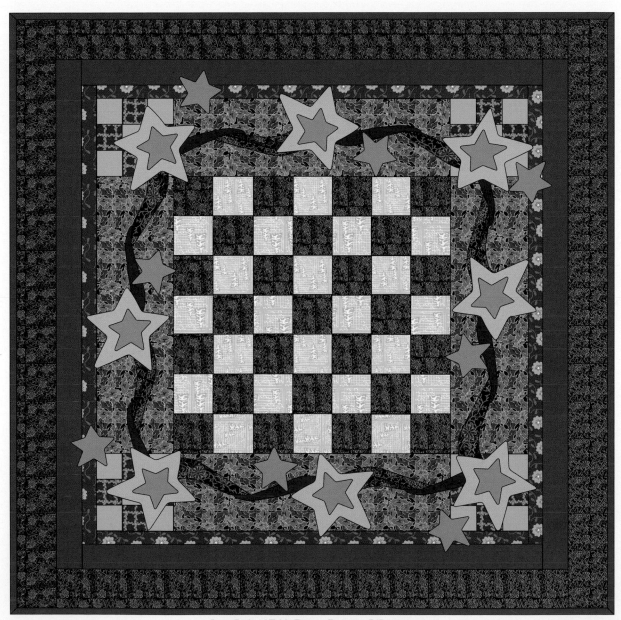

Star Garland Table Topper Diagram, 54" square

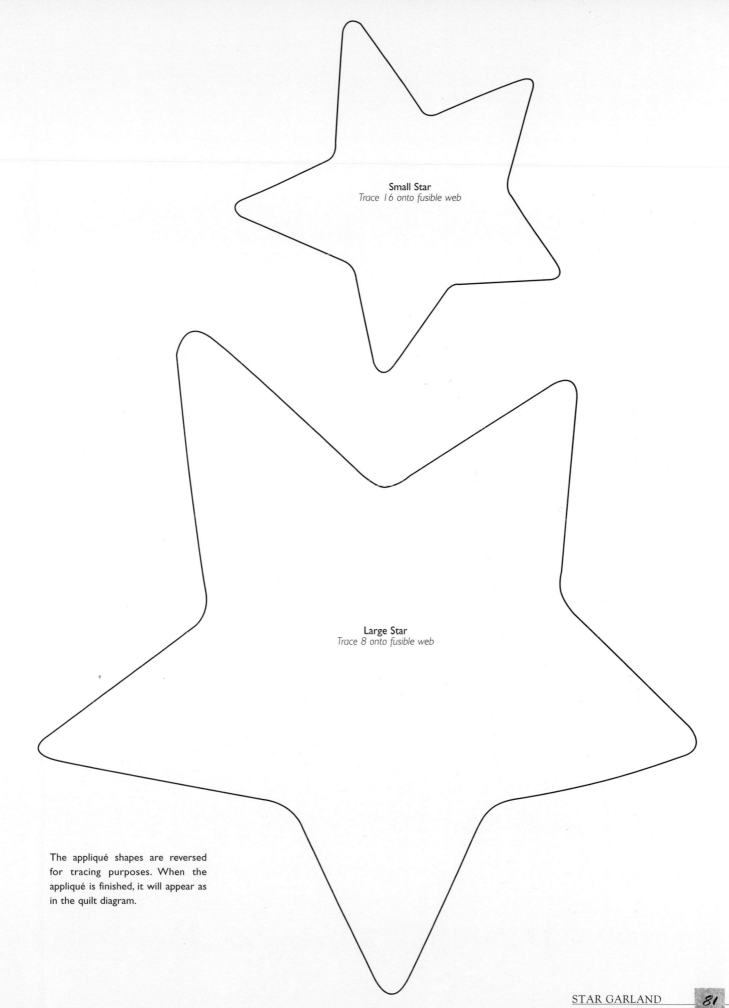

Small Star
Trace 16 onto fusible web

Large Star
Trace 8 onto fusible web

The appliqué shapes are reversed for tracing purposes. When the appliqué is finished, it will appear as in the quilt diagram.

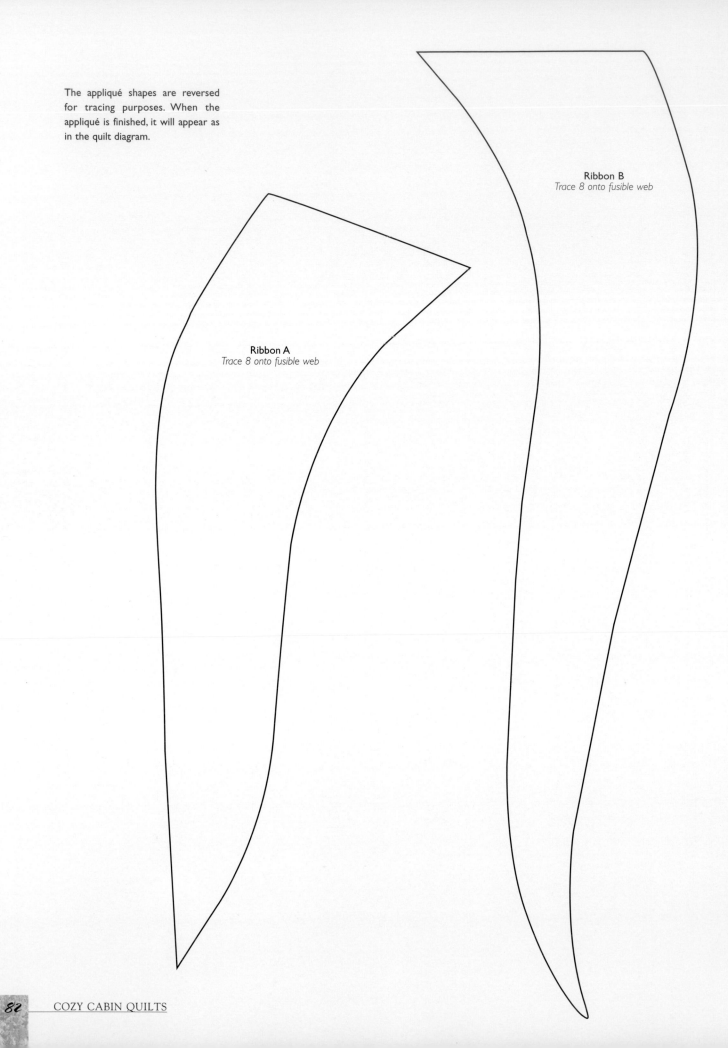

The appliqué shapes are reversed for tracing purposes. When the appliqué is finished, it will appear as in the quilt diagram.

Ribbon B
Trace 8 onto fusible web

Ribbon A
Trace 8 onto fusible web

winter *Reflections* pillowcase

Fabrics and Supplies for One Pillowcase

We used flannel prints for the pillowcase and appliqués.

Yardage based on 42"-wide fabric

- ⅞ yard **red print** for pillowcase
- ½ yard **red grid** for trim
- One 9" x 12" piece **brown print** for gingerbread man appliqués
- Two 8" x 10" pieces **green print** for tree appliqués
- Two 2" x 5" pieces **chestnut stripe** for tree base appliqués
- One 4" square **gold print #1** for tree top star appliqués
- Two 9" squares **gold print #2** for large star appliqués
- Three 6" x 7" pieces **cream print** for snowman appliqués
- Three 2½" squares **solid black** for snowman hat appliqués
- Three 1" x 4" pieces **blue plaid** for snowman scarf appliqués
- 1½ yards paper-backed fusible web
- Template material
- Standard bed pillow form (20" x 26")

CUTTING

From **red print**:
Cut one 27" x 42" rectangle for pillowcase.

From **red grid**:
Cut one 13" x 42" strip for trim.

Special Measuring Instructions

If your pillow form size differs from 20" x 26", use the following instructions to determine the correct size to cut your pillowcase rectangle.

Measure the distance around the middle of your pillow form, and add 1" to the measurement to allow for a ½" seam allowance.

Measure the length of your pillow form, and add 1" to the measurement to allow for a ½" seam allowance at each end of the pillowcase.

Fusible Web Appliqué

Step 1
Make templates using the patterns on pages 85-87.

Step 2
Position the templates on the fusible web, paper side up, making sure the shapes are at least ½"

apart. With a pencil, trace the shapes the number of times as indicated on each pattern. Cut the shapes apart leaving a small margin beyond the drawn lines.

NOTE: When you are fusing a large shape like the large star, fuse just the outer edges of the shape so that it will not look stiff when finished. To do this, draw a line about ⅜" inside the star, and cut away the fusible web on this line.

Step 3
Following the manufacturer's instructions, fuse the shapes to the wrong side of the fabrics chosen for the appliqués. Let the fabric cool and cut along the traced line. Peel away the paper backing.

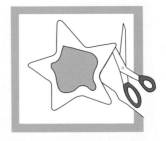

Step 4

Referring to the pillowcase diagram, position the shapes on the pillowcase, layering as needed, and pin in place. With matching thread, machine-zigzag stitch the appliqués in place. With black thread, machine-cross stitch the snowman's buttons.

Pillowcase Diagram

Assemble the Pillowcase

Step 1

Fold the 13" x 42" **red grid** trim strip in half lengthwise with wrong sides together and press. *At this point the trim strip should measure 6½" x 42".*

Step 2

With right sides together and raw edges even, stitch the 6½"-wide **red grid** trim strip to the 42" side of the **red print** rectangle using a ½" seam allowance. Press the seam allowance toward the **red grid** trim strip.

Step 3

With right sides together, fold the pillowcase in half crosswise and sew the raw edges together using a ½" seam allowance and press.

Step 4

Turn the folded edge of the trim to the wrong side of the **red print** fabric so that the stitching line does not show. Press, pin in place, and topstitch the trim in place. Turn the pillowcase right side out and insert the pillow form.

Hat
Trace 3 onto fusible web

The appliqué shapes are reversed for tracing purposes. When the appliqué is finished, it will appear as in the pillowcase diagram.

Snowman
Trace 3 onto fusible web

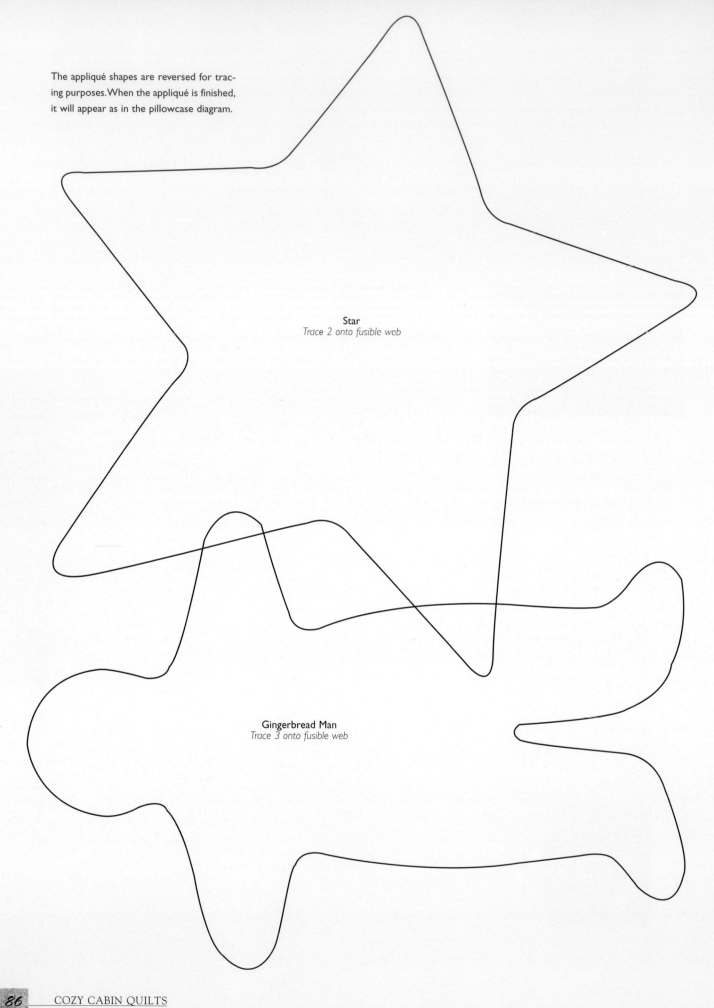

The appliqué shapes are reversed for tracing purposes. When the appliqué is finished, it will appear as in the pillowcase diagram.

Star
Trace 2 onto fusible web

Gingerbread Man
Trace 3 onto fusible web

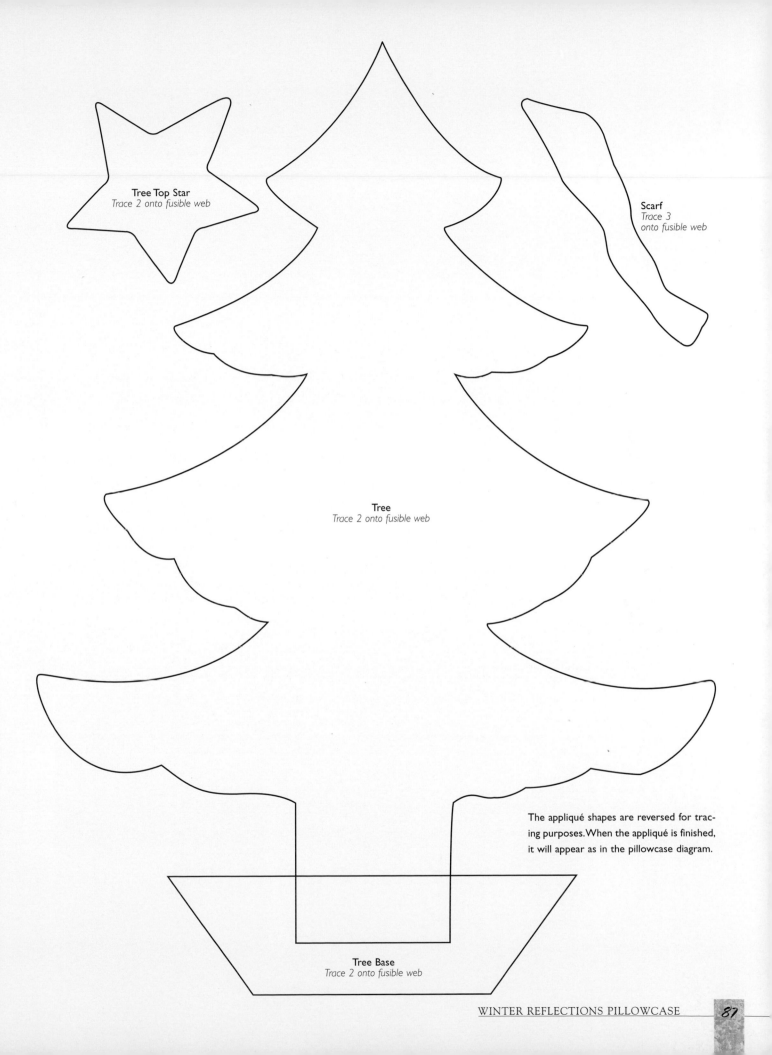

Tree Top Star
Trace 2 onto fusible web

Scarf
*Trace 3
onto fusible web*

Tree
Trace 2 onto fusible web

The appliqué shapes are reversed for tracing purposes. When the appliqué is finished, it will appear as in the pillowcase diagram.

Tree Base
Trace 2 onto fusible web

The "sound" of snowfall is serenity itself: silent and profound. When the snow ends, however, the fun begins. Better keep a quilt on hand for the après-ski warm-up.

Serenity

Peaceful *dreams*
come easily under a
comfy handmade quilt.

"Today's fast-paced *lifestyle* makes quiet time more *precious* than ever."

Checkerboard pines

Checkerboard pines

84" x 92"

Fabrics and Supplies

Yardage based on 42"-wide fabric

- 1⅛ yards **red print** for checkerboard quilt center, checkerboard border, and Four-Patch corner blocks

- 2 yards **beige print** for checkerboard quilt center, checkerboard border, triangle-pieced squares, and tree background

- ⅞ yard **green floral** for inner border, Four-Patch corner blocks, and large corner blocks

- 4 yards **dark green print** for triangle-pieced squares, trees, and outer border

- ⅛ yard **chestnut print** for tree trunks

- 1 yard **gold print** for middle border

- 2½ yards **tan/red plaid** for bias binding

- 7½ yards backing fabric

- Quilt batting, at least 88" x 96"

Checkerboard Quilt Center

CUTTING FOR CHECKERBOARD QUILT CENTER AND BORDER

From **red print** and **beige print**:
Cut seven 4½" x 42" strips each.

PIECING

Step 1

Aligning long edges, sew the 4½" x 42" **red print** and **beige print** strips together in pairs, and press toward the **red print** strip. Make 7 strip sets. Cut the strip sets into segments. Note: Set 26 segments aside to be used in the checkerboard border.

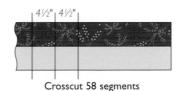

Crosscut 58 segments

Step 2

Referring to the checkerboard quilt center diagram for placement, sew 9 of the Step 1 segments together, alternating the colors and press. Make 3 rows of 9 segments each.

Step 3

Referring to the checkerboard quilt center diagram for placement, sew 5 of the Step 1 segments together, alternating the colors and press.

Remove one **beige** square from the row of 5 segments.

Checkerboard
Quilt Center Diagram

Step 4

Sew the 4 rows together, matching the seam intersections, and press. *At this point the checkerboard quilt center should measure 28½" x 36½".*

Inner Border

CUTTING

From **green floral**:
Cut four 2½" x 42" inner border strips.

ATTACHING THE BORDERS

To attach the 2½"-wide **green floral** inner border strips, refer to page 139 for complete Border instructions.

to page 139 for complete Border instructions.

Tree/Triangle-Pieced Square/Four-Patch Corner Block Borders

Make 10 Tree blocks, 8 triangle-pieced squares, and 4 Four-Patch corner blocks.

CUTTING

From dark green print:

Cut one 8⅞" x 42" strip.

Cut three 4½" x 42" strips. From these strips cut ten 4½" x 8½" rectangles.

Cut three 2½" x 42" strips. From these strips cut ten 2½" x 8½" rectangles.

From beige print:

Cut one 8⅞" x 42" strip.

Cut three 4½" x 42" strips. From these strips cut twenty 4½" squares.

Cut two 2½" x 42" strips. From these strips cut twenty 2½" squares.

Cut two 3½" x 42" strips.

From chestnut print:

Cut one 2½" x 42" strip.

From red print and green floral:

Cut one 4½" x 42" strip each.

PIECING

Step 1

With right sides together, layer the 8⅞" x 42" **dark green** and **beige** strips in pairs. Press together, but do not sew. Cut the layered strips into four 8⅞" squares. Cut the layered squares in half diagonally to make 8 sets of triangles. Stitch ¼" from the diagonal edge of each pair of triangles and press. *At this point each triangle-pieced square should measure 8½" square.*

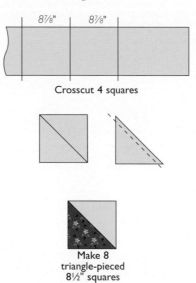

Crosscut 4 squares

Make 8 triangle-pieced 8½" squares

Step 2

Position a 4½" **beige** square on the corner of a 4½" x 8½" **dark green** rectangle. Draw a diagonal line on the **beige** square and stitch on the line. Trim the seam allowance to

¼" and press. Repeat this process at the opposite corner of the **dark green** rectangle.

Make 10

Step 3

Position 2½" **beige** squares on both corners of a 2½" x 8½" **dark green** rectangle. Draw a diagonal line on the **beige** squares and stitch on the lines. Trim the seam allowances to ¼" and press.

Make 10

Step 4

Aligning long edges, sew one 3½" x 42" **beige** strip to both sides of the 2½" x 42" **chestnut** strip and press. Cut the strip set into segments.

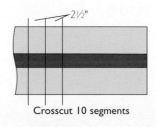

Crosscut 10 segments

Step 5

Referring to the Tree block diagram, sew the tree units together and press. *At this point each Tree block should measure 8½" square.*

Make 10

Step 6

Aligning long edges, sew the 4½" x 42" **red print** and **green floral** strips together and press. Cut the strip set into segments. Sew the segments together in pairs and press.

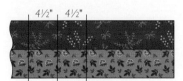

4½"   4½"

Crosscut 8 segments

Make four
8½" Four-
Patch corners

Step 7

For the top and bottom borders, refer to the quilt diagram and sew together 2 of the Tree blocks and 2 of the triangle-pieced squares and press. *At this point each border strip should measure 8½" x 32½".* Sew the border strips to the quilt center and press.

Step 8

For the side borders, refer to the quilt diagram and sew together 3 of the Tree blocks and 2 of the triangle-pieced squares. Add the Four-Patch corner blocks to both ends of the side border strips and press. *At this point each border strip should measure 8½" x 56½".* Sew the border strips to the quilt center and press. *At this point the quilt center should measure 48½" x 56½".*

Borders

NOTE: The yardage given allows for the border strips to be cut on the crosswise grain. Diagonally piece the strips as needed, referring to page 140 for Diagonal Piecing instructions.

CUTTING

From **green floral**:
Cut four 8½" square corner blocks.

From **gold print**:
Cut six 4½" x 42" middle border strips.

From **dark green print**:
Cut ten 10½" x 42" outer border strips.

ASSEMBLING AND ATTACHING THE CHECKERBOARD MIDDLE BORDER

Step 1

For the top border, refer to the quilt diagram and sew together 6 of the checkerboard segments and press. *At this point the checkerboard strip should measure 4½" x 48½".* Cut a 4½"-wide **gold print** strip to this length. Aligning long edges, sew together the checkerboard strip and the **gold print** strip and press. Repeat this process for the bottom border. *At this point each checkerboard/ middle border strip should measure 8½" x 48½".* Sew the border strips to the quilt and press.

Step 2

For a side border, refer to the quilt diagram and sew together 7 of the checkerboard segments and press. *At this point the checkerboard strip should measure 4½" x 56½".* Cut a 4½"-wide **gold print** strip to this length. Aligning long edges, sew together the checkerboard strip and the **gold print** strip and press. Repeat this process for the opposite side border. *At this point each checkerboard/middle border strip should measure 8½" x 56½".*

Step 3

Add an 8½" **green floral** corner square to both ends of the checkerboard/middle side border strips and press. Sew the border strips to the quilt and press.

Step 4

To attach the 10½"-wide **dark green** outer border strips, refer to page 139 for Border instructions.

Putting It All Together

Cut the 7½-yard length of backing fabric in thirds crosswise to make three 2½-yard lengths. Refer to Finishing the Quilt on page 139 for complete instructions.

Binding

CUTTING

From tan/red plaid:
Cut enough 6½"-wide bias strips to make a 370"-long strip.

Sew the binding to the quilt using a scant 1" seam allowance. This measurement will produce a 1"-wide finished double binding. Refer to page 140 for Diagonal Piecing and Binding instructions.

Checkerboard Pines Quilt Diagram, 84" x 92"

Cider House mug mats
6" square

Fabrics and Supplies to Make One Mug Mat

- 4½" square of **beige print** for background
- 6" square of **gold print** for corner squares
- 4½" square of **tan floral** for background
- 4½" x 7½" rectangle of **green print** for star
- 3½" square of **red print** for center square
- 8" square of backing fabric
- Quilt batting, at least 8" square

Star Block

CUTTING

From **beige print**:

For the A triangles:
Cut one 3¼" square. Cut the square diagonally into quarters, forming 4 A triangles.

From **gold print**:

For the B squares:
Cut four 2½" squares.

From **tan floral**:

For the C triangles:
Cut one 3¼" square. Cut the square diagonally into quarters, forming 4 C triangles.

From **green print**:

For the D triangles:
Cut two 3¼" squares. Cut the squares diagonally into quarters, forming 8 D triangles.

From **red print**:

For the E square:
Cut one 2½" square.

PIECING

Step 1

Layer a D triangle on an A triangle. Stitch along the bias edge as shown, being careful not to stretch the triangles, and press. Repeat for 3 more D and A triangles. Make sure you sew with the D triangle on top, and sew along the same bias edge of each triangle set so that your pieced triangle units will all have the D triangle on the same side.

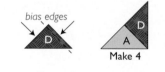

bias edges

Make 4

Step 2

Layer a D triangle on a C triangle. Stitch along the bias edge as shown, being careful not to stretch the triangles, and press. Repeat for 3 more D and C triangles. Make sure you sew with the D triangle on top, and sew along the same bias edge of each triangle set so that your pieced triangle units will all have the D triangle on the same side.

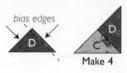

bias edges

Make 4

Step 3

Sew the Step 1 and Step 2 triangle units together and press. *At this point the star point unit should measure 2½" square.*

Make 4

Step 4

Sew a 2½" B square to both sides of a Step 3 star point unit and press.

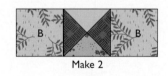

Make 2

Step 5

Sew a star point unit to both sides of a 2½" E square and press.

Make 1

Step 6

Sew the Step 4 units to both sides of the Step 5 unit and press. *At this point the star block should measure 6½" square.*

Make 1

Step 7

Layer the batting, backing, and star block, right sides together. Sew ¼" from the cut edges, leaving 3" open on one side.

Step 8

Trim the backing to ¼" and trim the batting to the seam line. Turn the mug mat right side out, and press, taking care to see that the corners are sharp and even.

Step 9

Handstitch the opening closed.

Cider House
tablecloth

Cider House
54" square **tablecloth**

Fabrics and Supplies
Yardage based on 42"-wide fabric

- 1¼ yards **beige print** for tablecloth center
- Thirty-two 7½" squares of **assorted prints** for border squares
- 3⅓ yards backing fabric

Tablecloth Top
CUTTING
From **beige print:**
Cut one 42½" center square.

From **assorted prints:**
Cut a total of thirty-two 6½" squares.

PIECING
Step 1
For the top and bottom borders, sew together 7 of the 6½" **assorted print** squares and press. Make 2 border strips. Sew the borders to the top and bottom of the 42½" **beige** square and press.

Step 2
For the side borders, sew together 9 of the **assorted print** 6½" squares and press. Make 2 border strips. Sew the borders to the sides of the **beige** square.

Putting It All Together
Step 1
Cut the 3⅓-yard length of backing fabric in half crosswise to make two 1⅔-yard lengths. Sew the long edges together and press. Trim the backing to the size of the tablecloth.

Step 2
With right sides together, layer the pieced tablecloth top and the backing. Sew the layers together ¼" from the raw edges, leaving 4" open on one side for turning.

Step 3
Clip the corner seam allowances and turn the tablecloth right side out. Press, making sure the corners are sharp and even. Handstitch the opening closed.

Step 4
Topstitch ½" away from the edge of the tablecloth.

Star Sled quilt

Star Sled
54" x 70" **quilt**

Fabrics and Supplies

Yardage based on 42"-wide fabric

- 2½ yards **red print** for center rectangle, middle borders, outer border, and star appliqués
- ⅞ yard **green solid** for inner border and middle border
- 1¾ yards **beige print** for middle border and star appliqués
- ⅞ yard **green grid** for middle border
- 1⅝ yards **tan/red plaid** for bias binding
- 3⅓ yards backing fabric
- Quilt batting, at least 58" x 74"
- Black pearl cotton for decorative stitches
- Template material
- 2 yards paper-backed fusible web for appliqués

Quilt Top

NOTE: The yardage given allows for the strips to be cut on the crosswise grain. Diagonally piece the strips as needed, referring to page 140 for Diagonal Piecing instructions.

CUTTING

From red print:
Cut one 10½" x 26½" rectangle.

Cut three 4½" x 42" strips. From these strips cut two 4½" x 38½" strips for wide middle border and two 4½" x 14½" strips for wide middle border.

Cut seven more 4½" x 42" strips. From these strips cut two 4½" x 70½" strips for outer border and two 4½" x 46½" strips for outer border.

Cut six 2½" x 42" strips. From these strips cut two 2½" x 58½" strips for narrow middle border and two 2½" x 38½" strips for narrow middle border.

From green solid:
Cut three 2½" x 42" strips. From these strips cut two 2½" x 30½" strips for inner border and two 2½" x 10½" strips for inner border.

Cut six more 2½" x 42" strips. From these strips cut two 2½" x 62½" strips for middle border and two 2½" x 42½" strips for middle border.

From beige print:
Cut four 4½" x 42" strips. From these strips cut two 4½" x 46½" strips for middle border and two 4½" x 22½" strips for middle border.

From green grid:
Cut five 4½" x 42" strips. From these strips cut two 4½" x 54½" strips for middle border and two 4½" x 30½" strips for middle border.

QUILT TOP ASSEMBLY

Step 1
Sew the 2½" x 10½" **green solid** strips to the top and bottom of the 10½" x 26½" **red** rectangle and press. Sew the 2½" x 30½" **green solid** strips to the sides of the rectangle and press.

Step 2
Sew the 4½" x 14½" **red** strips to the top and bottom of the quilt top and press. Sew the 4½" x 38½" **red** strips to the sides of the quilt top and press.

Step 3
Sew the 4½" x 22½" **beige** strips to the top and bottom of the quilt top and press. Sew the 4½" x 46½" **beige** strips to the sides of the quilt top and press.

Step 4
Sew the 4½" x 30½" **green grid** strips to the top and bottom of the quilt top and press. Sew the 4½" x 54½" **green grid** strips to the sides of the quilt top and press.

Step 5

Sew the 2½" x 38½" **red** strips to the top and bottom of the quilt top and press. Sew the 2½" x 58½" **red** strips to the sides of the quilt top and press.

Step 6

Sew the 2½" x 42½" **green solid** strips to the top and bottom of the quilt top and press. Sew the 2½" x 62½" **green solid** strips to the sides of the quilt top and press.

Step 7

Sew the 4½" x 46½" **red** strips to the top and bottom of the quilt top and press. Sew the 4½" x 70½" **red** strips to the sides of the quilt top and press.

Fusible Web Appliqué

PREPARE THE STARS

Step 1

Make templates using the large star and small star patterns on page 105.

Step 2

Position the templates on the fusible web, paper side up, making sure the shapes are at least ½" apart. With a pencil, trace the shapes the number of times indicated on each pattern, leaving a small margin between each shape. Cut the shapes apart.

NOTE: When you are fusing a large shape like the star, fuse just the outer edges of the shape, so that it will not look stiff when finished. To do this, draw a line about ⅜" inside

the star, and cut away the fusible web on this line, as shown.

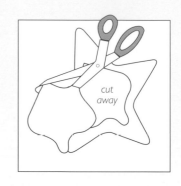

Step 3

Following the manufacturer's instructions, fuse the shapes to the wrong side of the fabrics chosen for the appliqués. Let the fabric cool and cut along the traced line of each shape. Peel away the paper backing.

Step 4

Referring to the quilt diagram, position the appliqué shapes on the quilt top and fuse in place. Buttonhole-stitch around the star shapes using black pearl cotton.

NOTE: To prevent the Buttonhole stitches from "rolling off" the edges of the appliqué shapes take an extra back stitch in the same place as you made the Buttonhole stitch, going around outer curves, corners, and points. For straight edges, taking a back stitch every inch is enough.

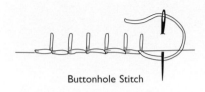

Buttonhole Stitch

Putting It All Together

Cut the 3⅓-yard length of backing fabric in half crosswise to make two 1⅔-yard lengths. Refer to Finishing the Quilt on page 139 for complete instructions.

Binding

CUTTING

From **tan/red plaid**:

Cut enough 6½"-wide bias strips to make a 270"-long strip. Sew the binding to the quilt using a scant ⅞" seam allowance. This measurement will produce a 1"-wide finished double binding. Refer to page 140 for Diagonal Piecing and Binding instructions.

Small Star
Trace 12 onto fusible web

Large Star
Trace 12 onto fusible web

Star Sled Quilt Diagram, 54" x 70"

winter
Splendor

winter Splendor

73" x 91"
Block: 15" square (finished)

Fabrics and Supplies

Yardage based on 42"-wide fabric

- 3 yards **beige print** for blocks and pieced border
- 2½ yards **red print** for blocks, lattice strips, and pieced border
- 2¼ yards **dark green print** for nine-patch units, lattice strips, and corner blocks
- ⅜ yard **chestnut/black grid** for lattice posts
- 1½ yards **green floral** for outer border
- ⅞ yard **red print** for binding
- 5⅓ yards backing fabric
- Quilt batting, at least 77" x 95"

Pieced Blocks

Make 12 blocks.

CUTTING

From **beige print**:
Cut eight 3⅞" x 42" strips.

Cut six 3½" x 42" strips. From these strips cut sixty 3½" squares.

Cut eighteen 1½" x 42" strips.

From **red print**:
Cut eight 3⅞" x 42" strips.

Cut five 1½" x 42" strips.

From **dark green print**:
Cut ten 1½" x 42" strips.

PIECING

Step 1

With right sides together, layer the 3⅞" x 42" **beige** and **red** strips in pairs. Press together, but do not sew. Cut the layered strips into squares. Cut the layered squares in half diagonally to make 144 sets of triangles. Stitch ¼" from the diagonal edge of each pair of triangles and press. *At this point each triangle-pieced square should measure 3½" square.*

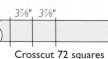

Crosscut 72 squares

Make 144
triangle-pieced
3½" squares

Step 2

Sew together 4 of the Step 1 triangle-pieced squares and a 3½" **beige** square and press. *At this point each section should measure 3½" x 15½".*

Make 24

Step 3

Sew a 1½" x 42" **beige** strip to both sides of a 1½" x 42" **red** strip and press. Make 5 strip sets. Cut the strip sets into segments.

Crosscut 48 segments

Step 4

Sew together 3 of the 3½" **beige** squares and 2 of the Step 3 segments and press. *At this point each section should measure 3½" x 15½".*

Make 12

Step 5

Sew a 1½" x 42" **dark green** strip to both sides of a 1½" x 42" **beige** strip and press. Make 4 strip sets. Cut the strip sets into segments.

Crosscut 96 segments

Step 6

Sew a 1½" x 42" **beige** strip to both sides of a 1½" x 42" **dark green** strip and press. Make 2 strip sets. Cut the strip sets into segments.

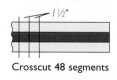

Crosscut 48 segments

Step 7

Sew Step 5 segments to both sides of the Step 6 segments and press. *At this point each nine-patch unit should measure 3½" square.*

Make 48
nine-patch units

Step 8

Sew together 2 of the Step 7 nine-patch units, 2 of the Step 1 triangle-pieced squares, and one Step 3 segment and press. *At this point each section should measure 3½" x 15½".*

Make 24

Step 9

Referring to the block diagram, sew the Step 2, Step 4, and Step 8 sections together and press. *At this point each block should measure 15½" square.*

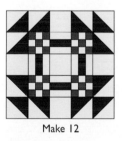
Make 12

Quilt Center

CUTTING

From **dark green print:**
Cut thirty-two 1½" x 42" strips.

Cut three more 1½" x 42" strips. From these strips cut eighty 1½" squares.

From **red print:**
Cut sixteen 1½" x 42" strips.

From **chestnut/black grid:**
Cut two 3½" x 42" strips. From these strips cut twenty 3½" squares.

PIECING AND ASSEMBLING THE QUILT CENTER

Step 1

Sew one 1½" x 42" **dark green** strip to both sides of a 1½" x 42" **red** strip and press. Make 16 strip sets. Cut the strip sets into segments.

15½"   15½"
Crosscut 31 lattice strip segments

Step 2

Position 1½" **dark green** squares on the 4 corners of a 3½" **chestnut/black grid** square. Draw a diagonal line on the **dark green** squares and stitch on the lines. Trim the seam allowance to ¼" and press. *At this point each lattice post should measure 3½" square.*

Make 20
lattice posts

Step 3

Referring to the diagram, sew together 3 of the Step 1 lattice strips and 4 of the Step 2 lattice posts and press. *At this point each lattice strip should measure 3½" x 57½".*

Make 5

Step 4

Referring to the diagram, sew together 4 of the Step 1 lattice strips and 3 of the blocks and press. *At this point each block row should measure 15½" x 57½".*

Make 4

Step 5

Referring to the quilt diagram, sew the Step 3 lattice strips and Step 4 block rows together and press. *At this point the quilt center should measure 57½" x 75½".*

Borders

NOTE: The yardage given allows for the border strips to be cut on the crosswise grain. Diagonally piece the strips together as needed, referring to page 140 for Diagonal Piecing.

CUTTING

From **beige print:**
Cut three 3⅞" x 42" strips.

Cut two 3½" x 42" strips. From these strips cut fourteen 3½" squares.

From **red print:**
Cut three 3⅞" x 42" strips.

Cut two 3½" x 42" strips. From these strips cut eighteen 3½" squares.

From **dark green print:**
Cut one 3½" x 16" strip. From this strip cut four 3½" squares.

From **green floral**:
Cut nine 5½" x 42" outer border strips.

ASSEMBLING AND ATTACHING THE BORDERS

Step 1

With right sides together, layer the 3⅞" x 42" **beige** and **red** strips in pairs. Press together, but do not sew. Cut the layered strips into squares. Cut the layered squares in half diagonally to make 56 sets of triangles. Stitch ¼" from the diagonal edge of each pair of triangles and press. *At this point each triangle-pieced square should measure 3½" square.*

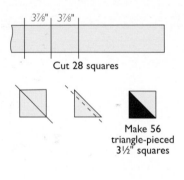

3⅞" | 3⅞"

Cut 28 squares

Make 56 triangle-pieced 3½" squares

Step 2

Sew the Step 1 triangle-pieced squares together in pairs and press.

Unit A
Make 14

Unit B
Make 14

Step 3

Sew together one Unit A, one 3½" **beige** square, and one Unit B and press. *At this point each section should measure 3½" x 15½".*

Make 14

Step 4

For the top and bottom pieced borders, sew together 3 of the Step 3 sections and 4 of the 3½" **red** squares and press. *At this point each pieced border should measure 3½" x 57½".* Sew the border strips to the quilt center and press.

Step 5

For the side pieced borders, sew together 4 of the Step 3 sections and 5 of the 3½" **red** squares. Add one 3½" **dark green** square to both ends of the strip and press. *At this point each pieced border should measure 3½" x 81½".* Sew the border strips to the quilt center and press.

Step 6

To attach the 5½"-wide **green floral** outer border strips, refer to page 139 for Border instructions.

Putting It All Together

Cut the 5⅓-yard length of backing fabric in half crosswise to make two 2⅔-yard lengths. Refer to Finishing the Quilt on page 139 for complete instructions.

Binding

CUTTING

From **red print**:
Cut nine 2¾" x 42" strips.

Sew the binding to the quilt using a ⅜" seam allowance. This measurement will produce a ½"-wide finished double binding. Refer to page 140 for Diagonal Piecing and Binding instructions.

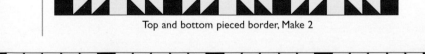

Top and bottom pieced border, Make 2

Side pieced border, Make 2

Winter Splendor Quilt Diagram, 73" x 91"

School's out and the cabin calls. Add a kaleidoscope of color to your vacation getaway with a quilt or two saved just for summer.

Vacation

Picnic days are *patchwork* days.
Bring along a *special* quilt.

COZY CABIN QUILTS

"Rainy day? *No problem!*
Involve the children (and grown-ups, too!)
in a *vacation memory* quilt."

Bluebird trail

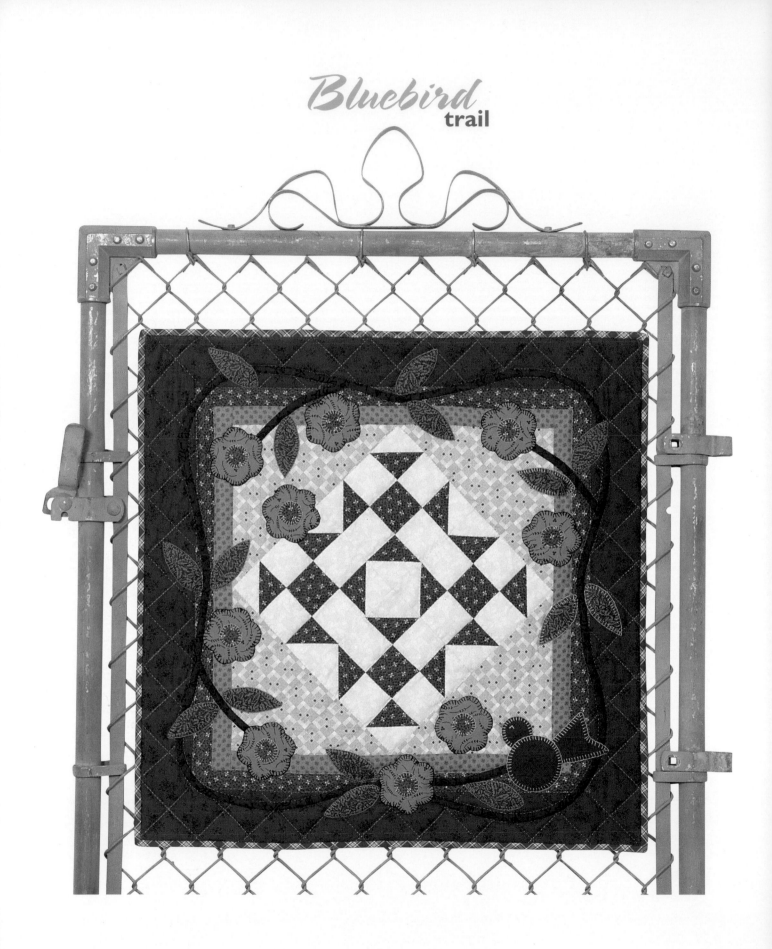

116

Bluebird trail

27" square

Fabrics and Supplies

Yardage based on 42"-wide fabric

- ⅜ yard **medium blue print** for blocks, middle border, and flower center appliqués
- ¼ yard **beige print** for block background
- 11" x 22" piece **tan grid** for corner triangles
- ⅛ yard **medium green print** for inner border
- ⅜ yard **red print** for outer border
- ⅜ yard **dark green print #1** for vine appliqués
- ⅛ yard **gold print** for flower appliqués
- ⅛ yard **dark green print #2** for leaf appliqués
- 7" square **dark blue print** for bird appliqué
- ½ yard **blue/yellow plaid** for bias binding
- ⅞ yard backing fabric
- Quilt batting, at least 31" square
- Template material
- ½ yard paper-backed fusible web for appliqués
- #8 black and gold pearl cotton for decorative stitches

Quilt Center

CUTTING

From **medium blue print**:
Cut one 2⅞" x 42" strip.
Cut four 2½" squares.

From **beige print**:
Cut one 2⅞" x 42" strip.
Cut sixteen 2½" squares.

From **tan grid**:
Cut two 10" squares. Cut the squares in half diagonally to make 4 corner triangles.

PIECING

Step 1
With right sides together, layer the 2⅞" x 42" **medium blue** and **beige** strips into pairs. Press together, but do not sew. Cut the layered strips into squares. Cut the layered squares in half diagonally to make 16 sets of triangles. Stitch ¼" from the diagonal edge of each pair of triangles and press. *At this point each triangle-pieced square should measure 2½" square.*

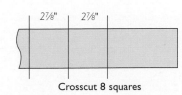

Crosscut 8 squares

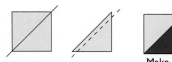

Make 16 triangle-pieced 2½" squares

Step 2
Sew triangle-pieced squares to both sides of a 2½" **beige** square and press.

Make 8

Step 3
Sew 2½" **beige** squares to both sides of a 2½" **medium blue** square and press.

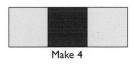

Make 4

Step 4
Referring to the block diagram, sew a Step 2 unit to the top and bottom of a Step 3 unit and press. *At this point each block should measure 6½" square.*

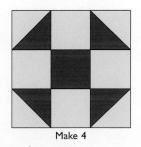

Make 4

Step 5

Referring to the quilt diagram for block placement, sew the blocks together in diagonal rows. Press the seam allowances in opposite directions so the seams will fit snugly together with less bulk. Sew the rows together and press. *At this point the quilt center should measure 12½" square.*

Step 6

Center and sew 2 of the **tan grid** corner triangles to opposite sides of the quilt center and press. Repeat with the remaining **tan grid** corner triangles.

Step 7

Trim away the excess fabric from the corner triangles, taking care to allow ¼" seam allowance beyond the corners of the quilt center. Refer to Trimming the Side and Corner Triangles on page 140 for complete instructions.

Borders

NOTE: The yardage given allows for the border strips to be cut on the crosswise grain. Diagonally piece the strips as needed, referring to page 140 for Diagonal Piecing instructions.

CUTTING

From **medium green print:** Cut two 1½" x 42" inner border strips.

From **medium blue print:** Cut three 1½" x 42" middle border strips.

From **red print:** Cut three 3½" x 42" outer border strips.

ATTACHING THE BORDERS

Step 1

To attach the 1½"-wide **medium green** inner border strips, refer to page 139 for Border instructions.

Step 2

To attach the 1½"-wide **medium blue** middle border strips, refer to page 139 for Border instructions.

Step 3

To attach the 3½"-wide **red** outer border strips, refer to page 139 for Border instructions.

Appliqué the Quilt Top
Vine Appliqué

CUTTING

NOTE: Diagonally piece the strips as needed.

From **dark green print #1:** Cut enough 1⅜"-wide bias strips to make a 90"-long strip.

Cut four 1⅜" x 8" bias strips.

PREPARE THE VINES

Fold each 1⅜"-wide **dark green #1** strip in half lengthwise with wrong sides together and press. To keep the raw edges aligned, stitch a scant ¼" away from the raw edges. Fold each strip in half again so the raw edges are hidden by the first folded edge and press. Set the prepared vines aside.

first fold

raw edges

second fold

Fusible Web Appliqué

PREPARE THE FLOWER, FLOWER CENTER, LEAF, AND BIRD APPLIQUÉS

Step 1

Make templates using the flower, flower center, leaf, and bird patterns. Appliqué patterns are on page 121.

Step 2

Position the templates on the fusible web, paper side up, making sure the shapes are at least ½" apart. With a pencil, trace the shapes the number of times indicated on each pattern, leaving a small margin between each shape. Cut the shapes apart.

NOTE: When you are fusing a large shape, like the flower, fuse just the outer edges of the shape, so that it will not look stiff when finished. To do this, draw a line about ⅜" inside the shape and cut away the fusible web on this line, as shown.

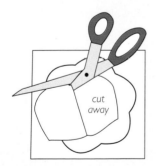

Step 3

Following the manufacturer's instructions, fuse the shapes to the wrong side of the fabrics chosen for the appliqués. Let the fabric cool

and cut along the traced line of each shape. Peel away the paper backing.

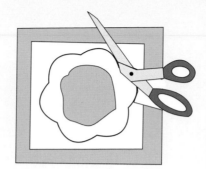

Step 4

Referring to the quilt diagram, position the vines on the quilt top, overlapping them as shown. Pin and baste in place, referring to the basting diagram below. Basting the vines in this zigzag fashion will hold them flat. Hand-stitch the vines in place with matching thread.

Step 5

Referring to the quilt diagram, position the appliqué shapes on the quilt top overlapping them as shown and fuse in place.

Step 6

Using black pearl cotton, Buttonhole-stitch around the edges of the flowers. Using gold pearl cotton, Buttonhole-stitch around the edges of the flower centers, leaves, and bird; Satin-stitch the beak; and straight-stitch the eye on the bird.

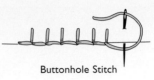
Buttonhole Stitch

Straight Stitch

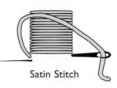
Satin Stitch

Putting It All Together

Trim the batting and backing so they are 4" larger than the quilt top. Refer to Finishing the Quilt on page 139 for complete instructions.

Binding

CUTTING

From **blue/yellow plaid:**
Cut enough 2½"-wide bias strips to make a 125"-long strip.

Sew the binding to the quilt using a ¼" seam allowance. This measurement will produce a ⅜"-wide finished double binding. Refer to page 140 for Diagonal Piecing and Binding instructions.

Bluebird Trail Quilt Diagram, 27" square

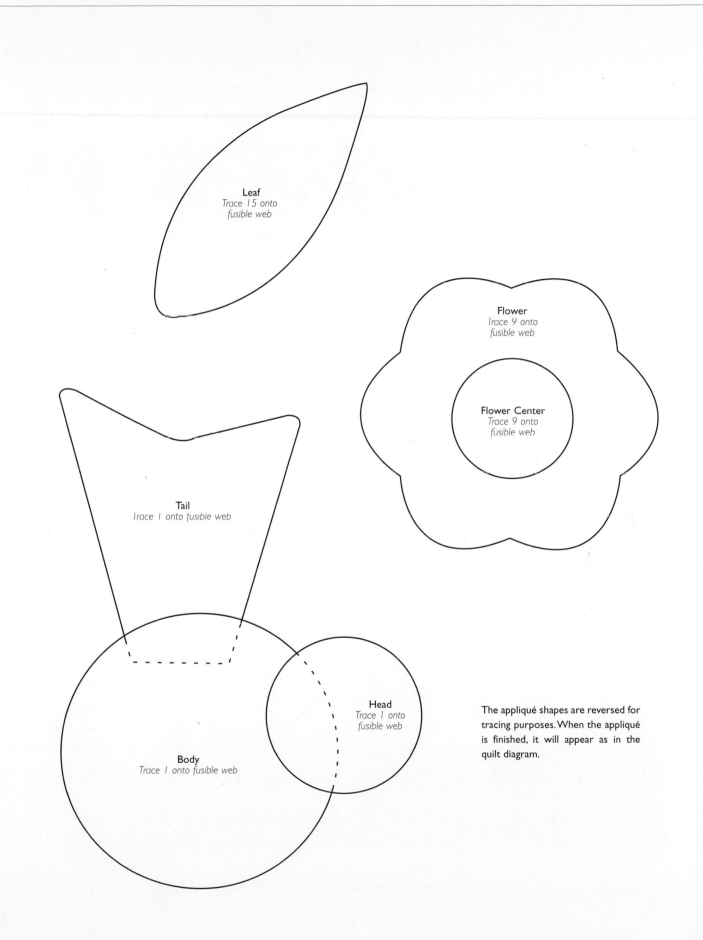

Leaf
Trace 15 onto fusible web

Flower
Trace 9 onto fusible web

Flower Center
Trace 9 onto fusible web

Tail
Trace 1 onto fusible web

Head
Trace 1 onto fusible web

Body
Trace 1 onto fusible web

The appliqué shapes are reversed for tracing purposes. When the appliqué is finished, it will appear as in the quilt diagram.

Bunk Mates

Fabrics and Supplies

Yardage based on 42"-wide fabric

Color Option 1:

- 3 yards **beige print** for blocks and inner border
- 2 yards **gold print** for Nine-Patch blocks and middle border
- 3⅛ yards **blue print** for triangle-pieced square blocks and outer border
- ⅞ yard **red print** for binding
- 5½ yards backing fabric
- Quilt batting, at least 78" x 96"

Color Option 2:

- 3 yards **beige print** for blocks and inner border
- 2 yards **blue print** for Nine-Patch blocks and middle border
- 3⅛ yards **gold print** for triangle-pieced square blocks and outer border
- ⅞ yard **red print** for binding
- 5½ yards backing fabric
- Quilt batting, at least 78" x 96"

Color Option 1
Nine-Patch Blocks

Make 54 blocks

CUTTING

From **beige print**:
Cut fifteen 2½" x 42" strips.

From **gold print**:
Cut eighteen 2½" x 42" strips.

PIECING

Step 1

Aligning long edges, sew 2½" x 42" **gold** strips to both sides of a 2½" x 42" **beige** strip and press. Make 7 strip sets. Cut the strip sets into segments.

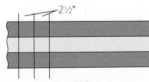

Crosscut 108 segments

Step 2

Aligning long edges, sew 2½" x 42" **beige** strips to both sides of a 2½" x 42" **gold** strip and press. Make 4 strip sets. Cut the strip sets into segments.

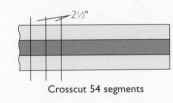

Crosscut 54 segments

Step 3

Sew a Step 1 segment to both sides of a Step 2 segment and press. **At this point each Nine-Patch block should measure 6½" square.**

Make 54
Nine-Patch blocks
6 ½" square

Triangle-Pieced Square Blocks

Make 54 blocks

CUTTING

From **beige print**:
Cut six 6⅞" x 42" strips.

From **blue print**:
Cut six 6⅞" x 42" strips.

PIECING

Step 1

With right sides together, layer the 6⅞" x 42" **blue** and **beige** strips in pairs. Press together, but do not sew. Cut the layered strips into squares.

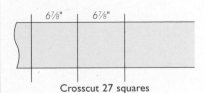

Crosscut 27 squares

Step 2

Cut the layered squares in half diagonally to make 54 sets of triangles. Stitch ¼" from the diagonal edge of each pair of triangles and press. *At this point each triangle-pieced square block should measure 6½" square.*

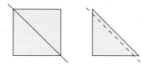

Make 54
triangle-pieced
6½" square blocks

Quilt Center

Step 1

Referring to the quilt diagram for block placement, sew the Nine-Patch blocks and triangle-pieced square blocks together in 12 rows of 9 blocks each. Press the seam allowances in alternating directions by rows so they fit together snugly.

Step 2

Pin the rows together at the block intersections and stitch. Press the seam allowances in one direction. *At this point the quilt center should measure 54½" x 72½".*

Borders

NOTE: The yardage given allows for the borders to be cut on the crosswise grain. Diagonally piece the strips as needed, referring to page 140 for Diagonal Piecing instructions.

CUTTING

From **beige print:**
Cut seven 2½" x 42" inner border strips.

From **gold print:**
Cut seven 2½" x 42" middle border strips.

From **blue print:**
Cut ten 6½" x 42" outer border strips.

ATTACHING THE BORDERS

Step 1

To attach the 2½"-wide **beige** inner border strips, refer to page 139 for Border instructions.

Step 2

To attach the 2½"-wide **gold** middle border strips, refer to page 139 for Border instructions.

Step 3

To attach the 6½"-wide **blue** outer border strips, refer to page 139 for Border instructions.

Putting It All Together

Cut the 5½-yard length of backing fabric in half crosswise to make two 2¾-yard lengths. Refer to Finishing the Quilt on page 139 for complete instructions.

Binding

CUTTING

From **red print:**
Cut nine 2¾" x 42" strips.

Sew the binding to the quilt using a ⅜" seam allowance.

This measurement will produce a ½"-wide finished double binding. Refer to page 140 for Diagonal Piecing instructions.

Bunk Mates Quilt Diagram, 74" x 92"
Option 1

Nine-Patch Blocks
Make 54 blocks

CUTTING

From beige print:
Cut fifteen 2½" x 42" strips.

From blue print:
Cut eighteen 2½" x 42" strips.

PIECING

Step 1
Aligning long edges, sew 2½" x 42" **blue** strips to both sides of a 2½" x 42" **beige** strip and press. Make 7 strip sets. Cut the strip sets into segments.

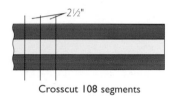

Crosscut 108 segments

Step 2
Aligning long edges, sew 2½" x 42" **beige** strips to both sides of a 2½" x 42" **blue** strip and press. Make 4 strip sets. Cut the strip sets in segments.

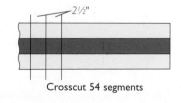

Crosscut 54 segments

Step 3

Sew a Step 1 segment to both sides of a Step 2 segment and press. *At this point each Nine-Patch block should measure 6½" square.*

Make 54
Nine-Patch blocks
6½" square

Triangle-Pieced Square Blocks

Make 54 blocks

CUTTING

From **beige print**:
Cut six 6⅞" x 42" strips.

From **gold print**:
Cut six 6⅞" x 42" strips.

PIECING

Step 1

With right sides together, layer the 6⅞" x 42" **gold** and **beige** strips in pairs. Press together, but do not sew. Cut the layered strips into squares.

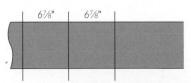

Crosscut 27 squares

Step 2

Cut the layered squares in half diagonally to make 54 sets of triangles. Stitch ¼" from the diagonal edge of each pair of triangles and press. *At this point each triangle-pieced square block should measure 6½" square.*

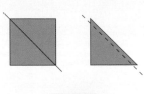

Make 54
triangle-pieced
6½" square blocks

Quilt Center

Step 1

Referring to the quilt diagram for block placement, sew the Nine-Patch blocks and triangle-pieced square blocks together in 12 rows of 9 blocks each. Press the seam allowances in alternating directions by rows so they fit together snugly.

Step 2

Pin the rows together at the block intersections and stitch. Press the seam allowances in one direction.

At this point the quilt center should measure 54½" x 72½".

Borders

NOTE: The yardage given allows for the borders to be cut on the crosswise grain. Diagonally piece the strips as needed, referring to page 140 for Diagonal Piecing instructions.

CUTTING

From **beige print**:
Cut seven 2½" x 42" inner border strips.

From **blue print**:
Cut seven 2½" x 42" middle border strips.

From **gold print**:
Cut ten 6½" x 42" outer border strips.

ATTACHING THE BORDERS

Step 1

To attach the 2½"-wide **beige** inner border strips, refer to page 140 for Border instructions.

Step 2

To attach the 2½"-wide **blue** middle border strips, refer to page 139 for Border instructions.

Step 3

To attach the 6½"-wide **gold** outer border strips, refer to page 139 for Border instructions.

Putting It All Together

Cut the 5½-yard length of backing fabric in half crosswise to make two 2¾-yard lengths. Refer to Finishing the Quilt on page 139 for complete instructions.

Binding

CUTTING

From **red print**:

Cut nine 2¾" x 42" strips.

Sew the binding to the quilt using a ⅜" seam allowance. This measurement will produce a ½"-wide finished double binding. Refer to page 140 for Diagonal Piecing instructions.

Bunk Mates Quilt Diagram, 74" x 92"
Option 2

Jacket Plaid

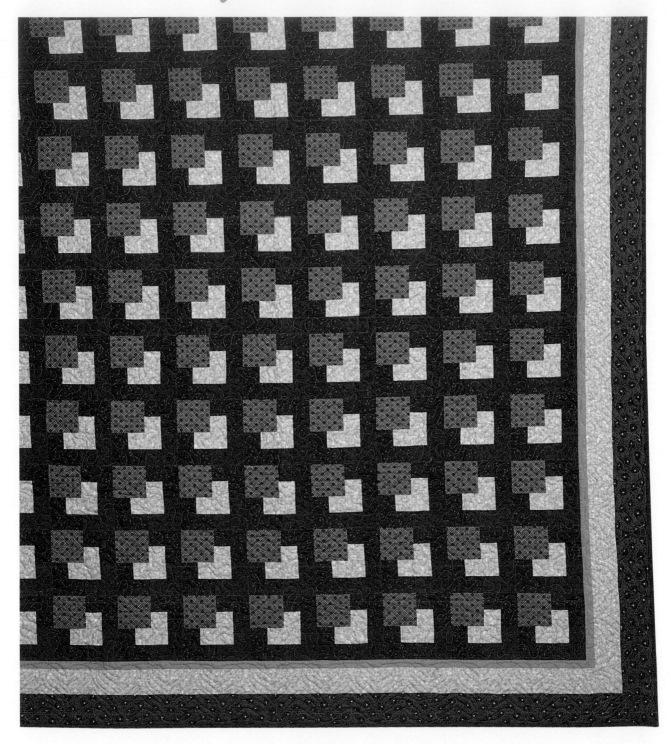

Jacket Plaid

88" x 96"
Block: 8" square (finished)

Fabrics and Supplies

Yardage based on 42"-wide fabric

- 1⅓ yards **red print** for blocks
- 2½ yards **dark blue print** for blocks
- 2¼ yards **tan print** for blocks and middle border
- 1½ yards **red grid** for blocks
- ½ yard **gold print** for inner border
- 1½ yards **medium blue print** for outer border
- ⅞ yard **red print** for binding
- 7⅞ yards backing fabric
- Quilt batting, at least 92" x 100"

Blocks

Make 90 blocks

CUTTING

From **red print:**
Cut six 4½" x 42" strips.
Cut six 2½" x 42" strips.

From **dark blue print:**
Cut six 4½" x 42" strips. From these strips cut ninety 2½" x 4½" rectangles.
Cut six more 4½" x 42" strips.
Cut twelve 2½" x 42" strips.

From **tan print:**
Cut six 4½" x 42" strips.
Cut six 2½" x 42" strips.

From **red grid:**
Cut ten 4½" x 42" strips. From these strips cut ninety 4½" squares.

PIECING

NOTE: The blocks are made up of strip sets. Refer to page 138 for Hints and Helps for Pressing Strip Sets.

Step 1

Sew the 4½" x 42" **red** and **dark blue** strips together in pairs and press. Make 6 strip sets and cut them into segments.

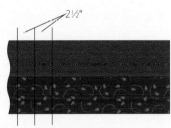
Crosscut 90 segments

Step 2

Sew a 2½" x 42" **red** strip to one long edge of a 4½" x 42" **tan** strip and press. Sew a 2½" x 42" **dark blue** strip to the opposite long edge of the **tan** strip and press. Make 6 strip sets and cut them into segments.

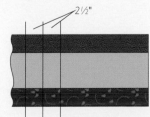
Crosscut 90 segments

Step 3

Sew the 2½" x 42" **tan** strips and the remaining 2½" x 42" **dark blue** strips together in pairs and press. Make 6 strip sets and cut them into segments.

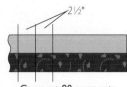
Crosscut 90 segments

Step 4

Sew a 2½" x 4½" **dark blue** rectangle to the right edge of a Step 3 unit and press. Sew a 4½" **red grid** square to the left edge of this unit and press.

Make 90

Step 5

Referring to the block diagram, sew the Step 1, Step 2, and Step 4 units together and press. *At this point each block should measure 8½" square.*

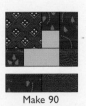
Make 90

Quilt Center

Step 1

Referring to the quilt diagram for block placement, sew the blocks together in 10 rows of 9 blocks each. Press the seam allowances in alternating directions by rows so they will fit together snugly.

Step 2

Pin the rows together at the block intersections and stitch. Press the seam allowances in one direction. *At this point the quilt center should measure 72½" x 80½".*

Borders

NOTE: The yardage given allows for the borders to be cut on the crosswise grain. Diagonally piece the strips as needed, referring to page 140 for Diagonal Piecing instructions.

CUTTING

From **gold print**:
Cut eight 1½" x 42" inner border strips.

From **tan print**:
Cut nine 3½" x 42" middle border strips.

From **medium blue print**:
Cut ten 4½" x 42" outer border strips.

ATTACHING THE BORDERS

Step 1

To attach the 1½"-wide **gold** inner border strips, refer to page 139 for Border instructions.

Step 2

To attach the 3½"-wide **tan** middle border strips, refer to page 139 for Border instructions.

Step 3

To attach the 4½"-wide **medium blue** outer border strips, refer to page 139 for Border instructions.

Putting It All Together

Cut the 7⅞-yard length of backing fabric in thirds crosswise to make three 2⅝-yard lengths. Refer to Finishing the Quilt on page 139 for complete instructions.

Binding

CUTTING

From **red print**:
Cut ten 2¾" x 42" strips.

Sew the binding to the quilt using a ⅜" seam allowance. This measurement will produce a ½"-wide finished double binding. Refer to page 140 for Diagonal Piecing and Binding instructions.

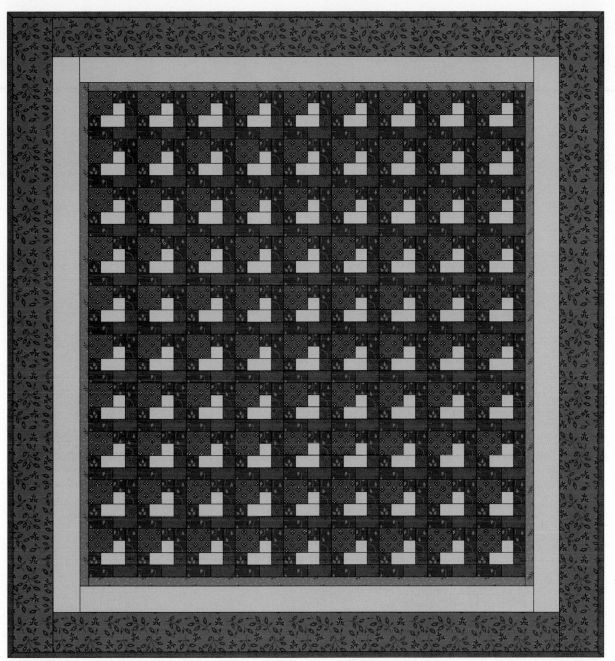

Jacket Plaid Quilt Diagram, 88" x 96"

Kid Art quilt

60" x 72"
Block: 12" square (finished)

Fabrics and Supplies
Yardage based on 42"-wide fabric

- 1½ yards **beige print** for blocks
- 1½ yards **red print** for log cabin strips and corner squares
- 1¼ yards **blue print** for log cabin strips
- 1¾ yards **red/beige plaid** for outer border
- ⅝ yard **blue print** for binding
- 3¾ yards backing fabric
- Quilt batting, at least 64" x 76"
- Permanent fabric markers for drawing
- Color crayons for drawing
- Freezer paper for stabilizer
- Water erasable fabric marking pen
- Brown craft paper

Blocks
Make 20 blocks

CUTTING
From **beige print**:
Cut five 10" x 42" strips. From these strips cut twenty 10" squares.

From freezer paper:
Cut twenty 10" squares.

From **red print**:
Cut twenty-six 1½" x 42" strips.

From **blue print**:
Cut twenty-six 1½" x 42" strips.

PREPARE THE BLOCKS
NOTE: Fusing a square of freezer paper to the wrong side of each **beige** square to stabilize it makes it easier for the little artist to draw on the fabric.

Step 1
With the water erasable fabric marking pen, mark an 8½" square on the right side of the **beige** square. The marked lines will be hidden in the seam allowances since the square is a bit larger than the finished block size of 8". This marked line helps the artist know how much area they have to fill with their drawing.

Step 2
Center a 10" freezer paper square (coated side down) on the wrong side of the 10" **beige** square. With a dry iron on the wool setting, press the squares together, fusing them. The squares are now ready to take on vacation.

NOTE: Pack markers, crayons, and prepared fabric squares in a plastic tote for easy travel. The cover of the tote can serve as a lap table for drawing while traveling. If you like, tape the fabric square to the cover to help hold it in place.

Step 3
Your little artist can now draw on the prepared squares with crayons and permanent markers. When the blocks are complete, remove the freezer paper, and press each one face down on a sheet of brown craft paper using a hot dry iron to set the colors.

Step 4
Trim each square to 8½" square. Lay out the blocks in an arrangement you like in 5 rows of 4 blocks each. Referring to the quilt diagram you will notice that the **red** and **blue** strips alternate in the log cabin strip piecing. You will want to piece the blocks using the correct log cabin strips.

Step 5
Starting with the block at the upper right corner of the quilt, sew a 1½"-wide **red** strip to the top and bottom of the 8½" **beige** square. Press the seam allowances toward the strips and trim the strips even with the edges of the square.

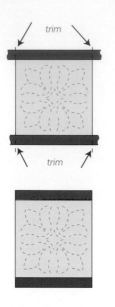

Step 6

Sew a 1½"-wide **blue** strip to the sides of the **beige** square. Press the seam allowances toward the strips and trim the strips even with the edges of the square.

Step 7

Referring to the diagram below, sew a 1½"-wide **blue** strip to the top and bottom of the **beige** square, press, and trim.

Step 8

Sew a 1½"-wide **red** strip to the sides of the **beige** square. Press the seam allowances toward the strips and trim the strips even with the edges of the square. *At this point each block should measure 12½" square.*

Make 10

Step 9

Repeat Steps 5 through 8, reversing the position of the 1½"-wide **red** and **blue** strips. Press the seam allowances toward each strip and trim the strip even with the edges of the square before adding the next strip. *At this point each block should measure 12½" square.*

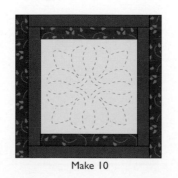

Make 10

Quilt Center Assembly

Step 1

Lay out the blocks in the planned arrangement. Sew them together in 5 rows of 4 blocks each. Press the seam allowances in alternating directions by rows so the seams will fit snugly together with less bulk.

Step 2

Pin the rows at the block intersections and sew the rows together. Press the seam allowances in one direction.

Border

NOTE: The yardage given allows for the plaid border strips to be cut on the lengthwise grain. Cutting the strips on the lengthwise grain will eliminate the need for piecing and matching the plaid.

CUTTING

From **red/beige plaid** (cut on lengthwise grain):
Cut two 6½" x 63" side border strips.

Cut two 6½" x 51" top/bottom border strips.

From **red print**:
Cut four 6½" corner squares.

ATTACHING THE BORDER

Step 1

To attach the 6½"-wide **red/beige plaid** top and bottom border strips, refer to page 139 for Border instructions.

Step 2

To attach the 6½"-wide **red/beige plaid** side border strips with 6½" **red** corner squares, refer to page 139 for Borders with Corner Square.

Putting It All Together

Cut the 3¾-yard length of backing fabric in half crosswise to make two 1⅞-yard lengths. Refer to Finishing the Quilt on page 139 for complete instructions.

Binding

CUTTING

From **blue print**:
Cut seven 2¾" x 42" strips.

Sew the binding to the quilt using a ⅜" seam allowance. This measurement will produce a ½"-wide finished double binding. Refer to page 140 for Diagonal Piecing and Binding instructions.

Kid Art Quilt Diagram, 60" x 72"

general

tructions

general Instructions

Getting Started

Yardage is based on 42"-wide fabric.

A rotary cutter, mat, and wide clear-plastic ruler with ⅛" markings are needed tools in attaining accuracy.

A 6" x 24" ruler is recommended.

Read instructions thoroughly before beginning the project.

Prewash and press fabrics.

Place right sides of fabric pieces together and use ¼" seam allowances throughout, unless otherwise specified.

Seam allowances are included in the cutting sizes given. It is very important that accurate ¼" seam allowances are used. It is wise to stitch a sample ¼" seam allowance to check your machine's seam allowance accuracy.

Press seam allowances toward the darker fabric and/or in the direction that will create the least bulk.

Rotary Cutting

"Square off" the end of your fabric before measuring and cutting pieces. By this we mean, the cut edge of the fabric must be exactly perpendicular to the folded edge, which creates a 90° angle. Align the folded and selvage edges of the fabric with the lines on the cutting board, and place a ruled square on the fold. Place a 6" x 24" ruler against the side of the square to get a 90° angle. Hold the ruler in place, remove the square, and cut along the edge of the ruler. If you are left-handed, work from the other end of fabric.

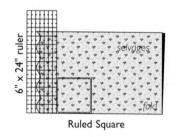

Ruled Square

When cutting strips or rectangles, cut on the crosswise grain. Strips can be cut into squares or smaller rectangles.

After cutting a few strips, if your strips are not straight, refold the fabric, align the folded and selvage edges with the lines on the cutting board, and "square off" the edge again and begin cutting.

yes

no

Hints and Helps for Pressing Strip Sets

When sewing strips of fabric together for strip sets, it is important to press the seam allowances nice and flat, usually to the dark fabric. Be careful not to stretch as you press, causing a "rainbow effect." This will affect the accuracy and shape of the pieces cut from the strip set. I like to press on the wrong side first and with the strips perpendicular to the ironing board. Then I flip the piece over and press on the right side to prevent little pleats from forming at the seams. Laying the strip set lengthwise on the ironing board seems to encourage the rainbow effect, as shown.

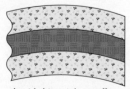

Avoid this rainbow effect

Borders

NOTE: Cut borders to the width called for. Always cut border strips a few inches longer than needed, just to be safe. Diagonally piece the border strips together as needed.

Step 1

With pins, mark the center points along all four sides of the quilt. For the top and bottom borders measure the quilt from left to right through the middle.

Step 2

Measure and mark the border lengths and center points on the strips cut for the borders before sewing them on.

Step 3

Pin the border strips to the quilt and stitch a ¼" seam. Press the seam allowances toward the borders. Trim off excess border lengths.

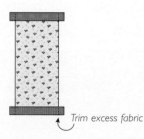

Trim excess fabric

Step 4

For the side borders, measure your quilt from top to bottom, including the borders just added, to determine the length of the side borders.

Step 5

Measure and mark the side border lengths as you did for the top and bottom borders.

Step 6

Pin and stitch the side border strips in place. Press and trim the border strips even with the borders just added.

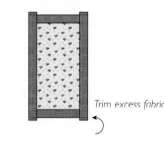

Trim excess fabric

Step 7

If your quilt has multiple borders, measure, mark, and sew additional borders to the quilt in the same manner.

Borders with Corner Squares

Step 1

For the top and bottom borders, refer to Steps 1, 2, and 3 in Borders. Measure, mark, and sew the top and bottom borders to the quilt. Trim away the excess fabric.

Step 2

For the side borders, measure just the quilt top including seam allowances, but not the top and bottom borders. Cut the side borders to this length. Sew a corner square to each end of these border strips. Sew the borders to the quilt, and press.

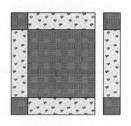

Finishing the Quilt

Step 1

Remove the selvages from the backing fabric. Sew the long edges together, and press. Trim the backing and batting so they are 4" larger than the quilt top.

Step 2

Mark the quilt top for quilting. Layer the backing, batting, and quilt top. Baste the three layers together and quilt.

Step 3

When quilting is complete, remove basting. Hand baste all three layers together a scant ¼" from edge. This basting keeps the layers from shifting and prevents puckers from forming when adding the binding. Trim excess batting and backing fabric even with the edge of the quilt top. Add the binding as shown on page 140.

Trimming Side and Corner Triangles

Begin at a corner by lining up your ruler ¼" beyond the points of the corners of the blocks as shown. Draw a light line along the edge of the ruler. Repeat this procedure on all four sides of the quilt top, lightly marking cutting lines.

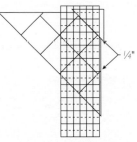

Mark cutting lines lightly ¼" beyond the points of the corners of the blocks.

Check all the corners before you do any cutting. Adjust the cutting lines as needed to ensure square corners.

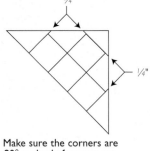

Make sure the corners are 90° angles before you cut.

When you are certain that everything is as square as it can be, position your ruler over the quilt top. Using your marked lines as guides, cut away the excess fabric with your rotary cutter, leaving a ¼" seam allowance beyond the block corners.

Diagonal Piecing

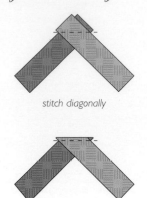

stitch diagonally

Trim to ¼" seam allowance

Press seam open

Binding

Step 1

Diagonally piece the binding strips. Fold the strip in half lengthwise, wrong sides together, and press.

Step 2

Unfold and trim one end at a 45° angle. Turn under the edge ¼" and press. Refold the strip.

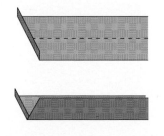

Step 3

With raw edges of the binding and quilt top even, stitch with a ¼"–1" seam allowance, as specified in the individual project, starting 2" from the angled end.

Step 4

Miter the binding at the corners. As you approach a corner of the quilt, stop sewing ¼" to 1" from the corner of the quilt. Use the same measurements as your seam allowance.

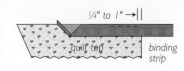
¼" to 1" →||
quilt top   binding strip

Step 5

Clip the threads and remove the quilt from under the presser foot.

Step 6

Flip the binding strip up and away from the quilt, then fold the binding down even with the raw edge of the quilt. Begin sewing at the upper edge. Miter all four corners in this manner.

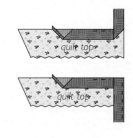
quilt top

quilt top

Step 7

Trim the end of the binding so it can be tucked inside of the beginning binding about ⅜". Finish stitching the seam.

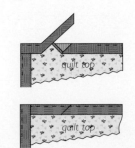
quilt top

quilt top

Step 8

Turn the folded edge of the binding over the raw edges and to the back of the quilt so that the stitching line does not show. Hand sew the binding in place, folding in the mitered corners as you stitch.

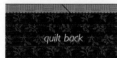

Index